THE
PRESSURE
GAME

KEVIN McSTAY

HEROBOOKS

THE
PRESSURE
GAME

KEVIN McSTAY
With Liam Hayes

www.**HERO**BOOKS.digital

HEROBOOKS

PUBLISHED BY HERO BOOKS
1 WOODVILLE GREEN
LUCAN
CO. DUBLIN
IRELAND

Hero Books is an imprint of Umbrella Publishing
First Published 2019
Copyright © Kevin McStay 2019
All rights reserved

ISBN 9781910827086

Cover Design and formatting: Jessica Maile
Ebook formatting: www.ebooklaunch.com
Cover photograph: Inpho
Inside photographs: Inpho, Sportsfile, Andrew Fox and the McStay family collection

◇ ◇ ◇ ◇ ◇

This book is dedicated to my beloved father,
Kevin McStay. He died on 3rd October, 2001.

He provided for his wife and his 11 children.
He helped shelter us, feed us, clothe us, educate us
and prepare us to 'leave the nest', a phrase he often
used. He did his best.

My father taught me right from wrong, that hard
work was an essential part of any success I might
achieve, that informing myself of the facts in any
debate was the starting point and that every person I
met along the way was entitled to fair play.

I don't think of him every day but I do think of
him most days. I loved him and I miss him.

◇ ◇ ◇ ◇ ◇

ACKNOWLEDGEMENTS

How did I end up agreeing to write this book? It's not like it was on my 'Things To Do List'. I guess Liam Hayes is to blame. He obviously uses the same sales pitch to all his subjects:

- Not an opportunity many people get
- Your experiences are unique
- It's a lovely legacy to your children and their children after them
- It's a chance to publicly thank those you love and those who helped you
- A book on the detail of Gaelic football management will be a must read

Good man Liam! The truth is I agreed to do this book because I trust Liam Hayes as a person and as a writer. So, I felt very comfortable from the start and took confidence knowing he would be in charge of the vehicle and would keep it between the ditches. Liam did the heavy lifting throughout and pushed me hard to make sure this book was an accurate and candid account of my three years in charge of the Roscommon footballers.

Senior inter-county management is a very difficult and demanding job. Outside the top five or six teams in the country, the reality is, on average, you generally lose more games than you win and if expectations for your group do not mirror these realities, pressure builds almost immediately.

We spent many hours in my home sifting through my memories in order to recall and describe those pressures. And this is the book that emerges from those interviews, emails, texts, chats, coffees and letters. Surprisingly, it has been a pretty good experience, causing me to reflect on many parts of my life which I'd placed in different compartments of my mind. And what unfolds is of course my truth. And I understand others will have, perhaps, a different version of that truth. But this is my truth and therefore the only one I could write about.

People that don't really know me tend to think my life runs according to a grand plan. If only you knew the reality. *The Cabal* (a WhatsApp group of my Cadet/army class friends: Rua, Coff, Skeff, Big D and Tim) would, I think, confirm pretty quickly that I actually stumble upon things, bump into opportunities. In other words, I've been very lucky in life. Things have fallen my way.

My career in the army was one such stumble. My mother got the application form and more or less filled it in for me. She knew instinctively, I believe, that I was drifting. I bungled along in the army not really focused on a career. I failed to complete career milestones in the expected timeframe. Just tipping away I suppose. Focusing on football when I should have focused on my career. Focusing on my career when I should have focused on my family. Pretty much doing things back to front.

My playing career for Mayo lacked real ambition; sure, I was happy to be part of it all but had no real sense that it was ever everything. Similarly, my RTE career, stints at journalism with *The Mayo News*, *Evening Herald* and now, *The Irish Times* came about because somebody contacted me, thought I might be decent at doing the thing they wanted and so, off I went. Tipping away. And for most of the things I did over the years, I was fairly good at the stuff without killing myself to be the best at that stuff.

I am grateful to a lot of people who helped to sort me out. My early teachers in primary school: the beautiful and kind Sister Carmel in The Convent NS; Jackie Clarke, Bro. Nicholas, Bro. Michael, Bro. Sebastian and of course my first great mentor, Mr. Tom Maughan in Scoil Pádraig.

I had a tough time at secondary school in St Muredach's College and as a result I gave up on my ambition to one day become a teacher in Ballina. But there were many decent human beings who taught there. I left at Easter in First Year and changed schools. In Ballina Vocational School my faith was very much restored. Mr. Quinn and Mr. Freyne provided the light. Daithi Quinn was from Tuam and became another mentor, teaching extra classes as required, encouraging me to improve and be the best I could be. When he departed to teach in St Jarlath's College in Tuam I was happy to follow him but devastated to leave 'The Tech' but worse, have to leave Ballina. Does that make sense?

Jarlath's was good for me and straightened me up a good bit. My much loved Auntie Eileen and Uncle Mícheál and the entire Hussey family in Airgloony, Tuam welcomed me into their home and I spent two very happy years there. On the teaching front I had Fr. Oliver Hughes, Fr. Dermot Moloney, Mr. Silke and Daithí Quinn (again). Men who taught and encouraged and corrected. The way teachers are supposed to.

I made two lovely friends there: Brian Moran and Conor O'Dea. Friends I don't see much of anymore. But they were great pals to me in the middle of my teenage years when I was trying to be cool around Tuam. I hear from them now and again. Somewhere along the journey we got busy with life.

The army then took over my life in the early 80s. My class officer was Capt. Paddy Moran and we got on famously. It was a tough time for sure in the Cadet School … nothing easy, nothing simple. Long hours, lonely hours. But that's all there was for me and I knew I had to make the best of things.

The late Dermot Earley was an army man I greatly admired. Tom Aherne too, an officer who influenced me as a cadet, a captain and a commandant when we soldiered together in The Curragh, later in the Western Brigade and finally, Defence Forces Training Centre (DFTC). In Lebanon and at home (DFHQ and Eastern Brigade) I worked with JJ O'Reilly, a very fine officer indeed. Tom Creaton and Ger Aherne helped me in so many ways, both at work and with St Brigid's GAA club. I remain friends with Pat McGreal over in Westport to this day – one of the cleverest and nicest men I met in the army. I had some excellent Commanding Officers: I was very fond of the late Jim Campion in Signals, and Mick O'Connor, a Rossie with a great sense of fun and friendship. And Gerry Hegarty was very good to me in Athlone and Lebanon. In Kosovo, my boss was Matt Murray and I had great time for him, too. Sincere thanks to all of you for helping me to tidy up my act.

Sean Kilbride, another ex-army man, continues to be a loyal friend, trusted adviser and supporter. We meet regularly these days for coffee, to talk over the issues of the day and exchange opinions. Like me, he is at heart a dreamer. Like me, he has lived both sides of the Mayo-Roscommon divide. We are both, I believe, much the better for it and I want to thank him for his support over the years.

Of course, the army has its full quota of gobshites too. You rarely had to travel too far to meet one. Just like any other profession, I imagine. But in general I met, admired and befriended so many excellent military people during my career.

My spiritual guidance is provided by another Rossie, the force of nature that is Fr. Pádraig Devine (SMA) who soldiers in the troubled lands of Kenya. You kept the faith when all looked lost to us, encouraged and supported and rejoiced in our successes. Thank you Fr. Pádraig.

Gaelic football has been a major part of my life and the love of this sport came from being a Stephenite and all that this great Mayo club stands for. My father, of course, played the primary role in inculcating a passion for the game in me but my coaches were also key influences: Gerry Kenny (St Pat's and the local Street leagues) was my first introduction to organised ball outside primary school. He was such an enthusiastic young coach and I loved togging for his teams. Tom Maughan (under-14s), Terry Reilly (under-16s) and Willie Casey (under-18s and under-21s) did some further polishing. I owe all of them, and the many others in that club, a debt of gratitude.

I've been involved with many clubs since I left Ballina Stephenites over 30 years ago. You learn that alongside the well-intentioned members of clubs there are others who deal only in negativity, pigeon-holing, back-stabbing and general apathy. But I always knew that Ballina Stephenites was very different. There was decency, fairness and only good intentions from the adults for the teams and the players of this wonderful club.

At county level I had four managers during my career. At under-16s I was managed by JP Kean, a former Mayo player I greatly admired. At minor there was the legendary Austin Garvan. And at the under-21 grade, John O'Mahony, who would go on to manage me at senior level also. But not before the manager who influenced me the most, Liam O'Neill, the former

Galway star. I must also name and thank Séamus Gallagher from Claremorris who was such a massive help in my formative years at team management with Mayo under-21s. Thank you all; the honour of wearing the Mayo jersey was not lost on me. You gave me that chance and when I wore those beautiful rich colours of the green and red jersey embossed with our county crest I did indeed feel special. To this day, our colours stir me deeply.

The Roscommon experience was, taken in the round, magnificent. Good days and bad, of course. Only to be expected. But being in charge of a county team that is winning matches is just such a high. We won some big games and had some great days. But the losses and the criticism were hard to take. Working at this level you come to realise the highs are high but the lows can be so damned low. The St Brigid's job was joy unconfined. The county job was tough. Just bloody tough. That's what happens all of us if we stay at sport long enough. We lose more than we win. It's the story of sport I guess. The story of life?

But I want to acknowledge all who soldiered with me at county level over the three years. I recall the vast majority of the players and back room team from that period very fondly. Liam McHale, Ger Dowd, Sean Finnegan and David Joyce provided the foundation and I will be forever grateful to those men. Dr. Martin Daly and Aisling Creighton led the medical team superbly and in the background Anthony McCormack (kit & eqpt) and Mick Byrne (statistics and any other job that was thrown at him) never tired working for our squad. But it is impossible to be all things to all men and so there are relationship breakdowns along the way. These things happen. We have to recognise them. And move on.

I want to acknowledge and thank our key sponsors Seán Mulryan (Ballymore), Tom Hunt (Ranger Pipelines), Dermot Hughes (Toyota) and another friend, Kevin Connolly (Roscommon/UK/Brazil) who supported me at every turn. Adrian Jones, an old army colleague from Tulsk, but now earning his crust in New York City, helped us dream that big things were possible. Anything these men could possibly do for us, they did it because they have a great passion for their county. And I want to thank the many, many Roscommon supporters who delighted in our successes and enjoyed the three years following us.

However, I want to reserve my greatest contempt for the sad haters out there and the erroneous stuff you wrote and spoke about me and my team, especially the online haters. You had few facts but big opinions, no idea what was going on but quick to fire a scud and insult us. Ye should be ashamed of yourselves but, of course, you are not. What sad lives you lead. No doubt this book will sustain you over the winter.

We have made Roscommon our home since the late 1980s. Our children, now young adults, were raised here; we are happy here and it is a grand town to live in. We have lovely neighbours in Hyde Court. During my three years managing Roscommon, they gave me such marvellous support. I want to especially mention Adrian Garvey, a former Roscommon footballer living beside us – your visits during the darkest days always helped. And you were right: there is life outside of football.

And I want to mention three other Mayo-Roscommon families who we befriended, whose children I trained, coached and managed and who in turn have been so kind and friendly to us: The Heneghan, McNeela and Kelly families. Like myself, service to the State brought you to Roscommon and it was here we poured foundations.

I want to acknowledge and thank lovely friends from the very start of my time living in Roscommon. Séamus Hayden, his wife Phil and his family have been a constant source of support. Séamus is a trusted confidante and wise owl. Without his advice and support I doubt I'd have stayed the course.

I want to thank 'The Traveling Wilburys': two close and dear friends - Seán Finnegan and Joe Gaffney. We've travelled the world together. And of course my old army friend, the larger than life Richard Coffey of Bantry. I think we met the first day we joined the army and have laughed most days ever since. Trying to boss us around the Cadet School during those early months was a member of our 'senior class' – Diarmuid Maloney (Godfather to our eldest daughter, Emma), a lovely lad from Galway. Thanks lads for your support, perspective but above all, unconditional loyalty over the years. It has meant a great deal to me. May we enjoy each other's company for many years to come.

From time to time I have lunch and sometimes a few 'weekend jars' with my Rossie mates, Declan Hoare and Ronnie McSharry and Sean Ridge from

Ballygar. But of course we don't meet up as much as we should. Once again, life just gets too busy and stuff does not get done. We must try harder fellas!

And so to my family. I adore my mother. What an incredible woman. I know everybody's mother is special but this Galway woman is just a fabulous lady. The most loving woman, the most caring woman, the most fun-loving woman I know. A woman with an enthusiasm for life like no other. Mam is now almost 88 years old and stays up later than most of us at family gatherings.

I love all my siblings dearly. But in a large family there tends to be breakaway republics and so Linda, the much loved sister ahead of me and Paul, the brother behind me, by virtue of timing, were the siblings I was most involved with growing up. The older gang were away in boarding school eight months of the year and the younger gang was, well, just too young to be hanging around with.

My younger brother, Paul is my best friend. The sibling I identify with the most. He is a loyal brother to me, deeply proud of me, I know. And me of him. He knows my every mood and move and makes allowances for them. A very clever and perceptive individual, we shared so much of our young lives growing up together. Not technically Irish twins – there are 16 months between us – but we were more or less reared as twins. We went everywhere together. An accomplished sportsman, Paul played Gaelic football with Ballina and Mayo, played elite level basketball and was an excellent soccer and snooker player. He is a very decent golfer. And a genius around cars. And windows.

My beautiful sister, Sinéad has always been a special presence. Married to my great friend, fellow dreamer and all round good guy, Liam McHale, she was always going to be part of the joys and the disappointments of the journey we've been on. I am grateful for all the kindnesses she has shown me and the Rossie McStays.

These days I work from home. I spend way more time with the beautiful girl I should have spent a lot more time with over the years. And I look out for my three beautiful daughters, Emma and our twins, Caoimhe and Megan. I'm so proud of our girls – grounded, bright, loving, caring, great fun to be around. Like their mother. Thankfully.

I want to also mark the contribution of Verona's parents, Howard and Vera, to my life. Thank you both for always picking up the slack, filling the gaps, helping out and advising us well.

I met Verona in July 1983 when I was an army cadet. I was just gone 21 and she would turn 17 a month later. We got married in August 1991 and have been together ever since. She is everything to me, to my girls, to this family. The glue that kept and keeps us all together. I know for sure that without Verona's influence in my 20s I would just have drifted. It would have ended up messy. Verona is such a calm, clever, funny, stylish, beautiful woman. She saved me.

I've lived such a varied life. A Mayo boy with Galway parents who settled in Roscommon. A most enjoyable football journey, a career in the army, a media career outside of it and now, finishing where I thought I'd start: teaching mathematics to Junior and Leaving Certificate students.

I've lived a very happy life to date. Even experienced joy a few times but mostly happiness, satisfaction and contentment. I never wanted to be anybody else. Just myself, happy in my own skin, tipping away at the things I like doing.

Some things worked out. Some things didn't. Like my Dad before me, I'm satisfied I tried my best at most things.

Kevin McStay
Roscommon Town,
September 2019.

PROLOGUE

'YOU SHOULDN'T BE in here... Kevin!'

'I know!' I replied.

'KEVIN!

'YOU SHOULD NOT BE IN HERE!'

'I know... I know that,' I admitted a second time, but I was already a fair bit into the room, and I could see the linesman sitting down to my right.

I turned slightly towards him.

'I am really sorry,' I told him.

But it was the referee I wanted, not the linesman. That was why I had knocked on the door. I was surprised that I was let in to be honest.

Niall Cullen was of no real interest to me. That was the linesman's name. I gave him his apology. That was that sorted. Now that I was standing in the middle of the small room it was the referee I really wanted. Ciaran Brannigan. A Down man.

What's a man from Down doing refereeing a game between Donegal and Roscommon?

'Ciaran!'

CHRISSAKES...IT'S THE SUPER 8s... it shouldn't be hard to get referees...

... at this stage of the season.

Get someone from Cork...

Kerry.

Anyone from Leinster.

'It was just a complete accident.

'It should not have happened, I know that... and I am quite calm about it now... and I apologise, Ciaran.

'I really apologise!'

I gave another quick turn of the head towards the linesman. Two apologies. Twice as many as he deserved.

'Okay!' Ciaran said, but I could see by the look on his face that he was not feeling all that okay. 'But... it's not acceptable for that to happen to one of my officials, Kevin!'

He wasn't happy.

Suddenly, I wasn't as calm as I had promised him. 'Do you realise, Ciaran...we're fighting for our lives out there!

'And that decision you just made out there... IT'S A KILLER.'

Calm it.

'Not to give us that free is a killer.'

He could see that I was still riled. I continued... though I remember thinking to myself... *he looks like he's sorry!*

'Ciaran... the whole stadium knows it was a free!'

'That's not the way I saw it,' he replied.

'How could you not see it?'

He was giving me a long, sympathetic look. 'I'm really sorry if it was a free, Kevin... I just didn't see it that way!'

I had nothing more to say to him. But I stood there. And he stood there. I know he is a good referee, and I know also that dozens and dozens of times I have said on TV when I am commentating on matches, that if the referee doesn't see something he simply can't blow that whistle. Referees don't refuse to give frees. Referees don't have any spite in them. I think!

How many times, I wonder, have I clenched my RTE microphone and reminded the whole country of that little fact. That managers are hot under the collar. That supporters are mad as hell, and that the coolest person in the whole place is usually the referee who is doing his level best to maintain law and order.

But I could not help wondering as I turned on my heels. Neither could I bin my paranoia.

What's Ciaran Brannigan doing refereeing Donegal? And that other fella?

He's an Ulsterman too... Fermanagh!.

I closed the door behind me.

Ciaran had actually apologised to me twice.

'If I missed it, I apologise Kevin!'

I wasn't expecting one apology, never mind two. I had a dressing-room to get back to. We were down five points.

Our second game in the Super 8s was as good as lost.

The 2018 season was right on the brink.

He had been all of the things I was not expecting him to be. He was rational and understanding of my situation as a manager in the deep end. He was also empathetic. He had told me he was human, and that he did not see what I saw. But, as I turned my back on him, he had also promised, 'I am going to have to take some action about what you did!'

'AHHH... COME ON!

'I've apologised,' I reminded him.

'I've said... I'M SORRY!'

◊ ◊ ◊ ◊ ◊

MY NAME IS Kevin McStay.

Same as my Dad. He married Maidie Holian and they had 11 children. I was their fifth. A boy in front of me died at birth, and he was buried as Patrick McStay because he was born in or around St Patrick's Day, I understand. I've also always been of the understanding that if he had survived he would have been called Kevin McStay.

Not me.

My Mum and Dad saved the name Kevin for their next boy. For me. When you are called after your father you feel a little bit of extra responsibility about that name. I've always felt that. There is something good about it. That responsibility just feels significant in a strange, underlying way.

As a reminder, my Dad would often tell me, 'Your name is not for sale!' He would say this to all of his children, but the resonance in his voice always left me in no doubt whatsoever that I carried a name that could never, ever, ever be sold.

Neither did my Dad like slobbering.

That was his word.

'Slobbering.'

He was a stickler at times. He had no time for messing of any kind. He liked his jar and he was happy to socialise, but he was not into... 'slobbering'.

As a kid when I tried out my fancy enough repertoire of different voices at the family table, my Dad was never very impressed. I might be doing a good Ian Paisley and mostly everyone else around the table would be laughing, but Dad saw it differently.

It was just 'slobbering'.

There were better things I could be doing than mimicking people off the television set.

As a boy in Ballina, everyone knew who I was and whom I was called after. My Dad was a post office official working in the heart of the town, and everyone was calling into him to get forms filled for God only knows what? He was an intelligent man, an informed man, a well-read man, someone others in the town knew as being a solid citizen.

Shouting at referees was slobbering, even though he practised it himself sometimes! Fighting with an opponent and getting sent off was slobbering.

Getting stopped by a Garda in the centre of the town, as I rode my bike home at 11 years of age, and had no light on the bike, that wasn't slobbering. But it was next of kin to a boy slobbering.

My Dad had bought me the light to keep me safe. Garda Moran was a friend of his. I knew they would share a pint one night and the name of young Kevin McStay would be brought up.

Guilty as charged.

◊ ◊ ◊ ◊ ◊

THE LINESMAN WOULDN'T stop to talk.

And what do you do when someone you want to talk with refuses to stop walking away from you? You reach out. You reach out and take hold of their arm.

He was entitled to keep walking.

I was very animated, but the incident between me and the linesman had passed off. There was a bit of a schmozzle on the field.

That passed off too. The half-time whistle had blown. Once the players had gone into the dressing-room we had our chat out on the field, as we always did. Liam, Ger and myself. We always took a couple of minutes out there, in the full glare of everyone in the ground but, at the same time, chatting out there offered absolute privacy.

I liked the players to have a few minutes alone to themselves in the dressing-room. There happened to be a ball at my feet. I don't know why, but I scooped it up with my hand and, yes, I did notice Ciaran Brannigan and his linesmen and umpires walking away together. They were about 10, maybe 15 yards away.

Again, it was not a conscious decision, but I realised that I had lobbed the ball up into the air in their general direction.

I imagined it hopping in the middle of them.

But then... as if in slow motion... I followed the ball as it descended. And I could see it was about to hit the linesman, or go damn close to landing on him. The linesman I had been having strong words with a minute or two before. The man I had grabbed by the arm.

Christ... it's going to hit him.

WE FELT THAT we had more than a fighting chance against Donegal, and that we could survive in the Super 8s for one weekend longer, at least.

We decided that we were going to have a more defensive unit on the field. That decision came in the hours after we had been hammered by Tyrone six days earlier in our opening game in the Super 8s.

It was Tyrone first in Croker.

Then Donegal in Hyde Park.

And, finally, The Dubs. Back in Croker! Three games in the Super 8s in four weeks. Roscommon, the only Division Two team still alive, in the deep end of the 2018 season.

We had two full sessions on the field to work on a bigger, tougher defensive unit.

Tyrone had scored four goals. But we were leaking too many goals before that, before Tyrone ran through us in Croke Park.

4-24 to 2-12.

It had been 1-10 to 0-6 at half-time. Seven points apart. Worse than that, the worrying part of that first-half scoreline was that we had got off to a decent start. We were one point in front. 0-4 to 0-3. Then in a flash, a piercing movement between Connor McAliskey and Cathal McShane was finished off by Niall Sludden.

That came in the 11th minute.

We steadied. After 22 minutes it was 1-4 to 0-6. Then? They shot six points without a single reply. Again, it was even worse than that. Six different men got those six points. It was like they were queuing up.

The story of the game?

You know that line from the movie, *The Untouchables*? Kevin Costner plays Eliot Ness, and he's listening to Jim Malone, who's played by Sean Connery, telling him how to get the crime boss, Al Capone.

'You wanna know how to get Capone?' Malone tells Ness. *'They pull a knife... you pull a gun. He sends one of yours to the hospital... you send one of his to the morgue.*

'That's the Chicago way!' Malone concludes.

The Tyrone way?

Those six fast points before half-time.

The three out of four scores coming up to the end of the third quarter, just when we had come back into the game with a goal from Enda Smith and a Diarmuid Murtagh point.

The three goals in the fourth quarter.

That's the Tyrone way.

Some of our more senior players got talking after the game and they asked me what was happening? What were we going to do about it?

In a week?

When we sat down as a management team, Liam, Ger and myself, that is what we asked ourselves. We were looking at one another and refusing to say aloud what we were all thinking.

What can we do in a week?

My own thoughts were that we had no choice. Liam and Ger were of the same mind. We had to do something fast.

But... in a week?

Why not a week? They're bright footballers.

We're not asking them to reinvent the wheel... well we are, but at the same time not really!

It is what it is. Smart footballers pick up things fairly quickly. We'll give them a framework. We'll work through it with them and we'll see how it pans out.

We'll work on it Tuesday, and again on Thursday and if it looks to be panning out... if we're happy enough?

We'll go with it on Saturday.

On the Tuesday, Liam went through it with them. We did it graphically, and then we did it out on the field, and we put it into action in a game. There was some frustration. Some of our defenders who were highly committed got agitated with others. A couple of lads went bananas. In the middle of it all, one defender stopped in his tracks and ripped through a forward.

'WHAT THE FUCK ARE YOU DOING?'

We could only instruct them. They had to work it out for themselves on the field aswell, understand instinctively who should be staying back in defence, and who should go bombing forward. By the end of the Thursday night they seemed to know what they were supposed to be doing in our new, hardened, tightened defensive unit. I was happy with them.

They're clever players.

We've looked at it on screen... and we've done it on the pitch. Twice.

They're not clowns.

They understand what they have to do.

At the same time, 48 hours before we would meet Donegal, I knew.

Of course I did, I knew that to bed in a defensive system you need a six months stretch of hard work on the field, and repetitive work.

You can ask the question: why hadn't we started working on a defensive system that would save us from the best teams in the country in the Super 8s, from Tyrone and Donegal, and Dublin, six months earlier?

It's a fair question.

Personally, I decided as team manager that we were not going to play that way. And I had good reason for believing this.

THE BALL LANDED on the linesman's shoulder.

I watched it slowly descend and... hit him.

Shit.

It was a 100 to 1 shot... make that 1,000 to 1, that the ball would land on the shoulder of the feckin linesman.

'The ball hit him, y'know?'

It was Liam who made that announcement, and who also decided to look into a crystal ball.

'You'll be in trouble for that... I'd say!'

I shook my shoulders. I said it would be okay, it would be fine.

'He'll make something of that... he's bound to!' The second voice belonged to Brian Carroll, the Roscommon county board secretary.

I said nothing.

But, I decided I'd go into the referee's room. I would tell them that I was sorry... *it was a complete accident! I threw the ball deliberately.*

But... I did not throw it at you deliberately.

That's what I'd tell them.

◊ ◊ ◊ ◊ ◊

I HAD ONLY two managers in my playing days with Mayo. Liam O'Neill and John O'Mahony. Liam was ahead of anyone else in the country in the mid 80s. But we were all 21 and 22 years old, and we were messing up and being eejits.

We were clowns at times.

It cost Liam the Mayo job. As players, we did not go about our business properly for him. Too many of us were slobbering. When we were ahead in matches, we were not driving it home. When we were behind, we were throwing in the towel. We were a hard bunch to manage. Then Johnno came in.

John O'Mahony was not the greatest coach in the game, but he was an outstanding manager. And he organised us, and he stopped us slobbering. We were three or four years older and we were willing to listen to him.

We knew what we had to do for Johnno, and we got to the 1989 All-Ireland final. Looking back all these years later, I feel I was lucky as a countyman. I had two very good managers. Alongside my Dad, they were two more men who were huge influences on my life, yet Liam and Johnno were completely different in nature and how they applied themselves amongst us. Liam was charismatic. Inventive in his thinking, always looking to be hands-on and instructive.

Johnno would not mix with us as players, but Liam loved being the boss of a winning football team and liked to stay close to his players after the game. Liam O'Neill was the first man in my football life who awakened me.

He brought me, and everyone else to our senses, even though we failed him with our immaturity. It was Liam who brought us in a VHS tape he had sourced in America. It was titled... *Bigger, Stronger, Faster.* He brought us to Limerick University to get us all fat tested. He told us we were going to be the best team in Ireland, and in 1985 we got to an All-Ireland semi-final and drew with Dublin, before going down to them in a replay.

Liam had a gym in Lacken for us, for those of us who were bothered to go into it. Never enough of us.

Johnno was meticulous. If you were hurt, he'd drive the length of Ireland to collect you and bring you to a physio and get you sorted. If you had no job, he'd get something done for you. He'd always have time for every last man. He was excellent in his man-management skills and figuring things out. He saw early that as a team we could do with a psychologist. Johnno ended up getting us two psychologists!

The story of Mayo football, I know that's what you're thinking. A team that needed head shrinks for decade after decade. Whether we needed them or not, Johnno had them on hand.

Great training locations.

As many footballs as we needed.

Hotels spot on.

A team bus that made you feel proud to be a Mayo man.

But, in terms of serious coaching on the field, there was not a lot going on in our camp. Back in those days, not many managers coached. And none of those managers brought an official coach into the set-up.

◊ ◊ ◊ ◊ ◊

IN MY DAY, we gave the ball away as fast as we got it. We'd kick it somewhere. It didn't worry us, because we knew we'd every chance of getting the ball back into our possession, 10, 20 seconds later. In the modern game, you don't get the ball back for minutes on end. You only get it back when the other team is finished with it. Or else, if you have made a big play.

The modern game is about aerobic fitness.

It's about the pair of lungs inside the footballer as much as anything else. It's about tracking. Pressure. Legal pressure and illegal pressure. Tackling and tackling.

And it takes a magnificently athletic team, from A to Z, to play the modern game to absolute perfection.

The Roscommon team I managed was not, as a physical specimen, on the same planet as Dublin and Mayo and the small handful of outstanding football teams in the country.

There were good reasons why.

BUILDING A DEFENSIVE structure does not require managers and coaches with degrees in engineering and architecture and science.

It's not hard.

Defence is easy. The hardest thing about building a winning team in this day and age is the offensive structure.

TO BEGIN WITH against Donegal we were outstanding defensively. We were minding our Ps and Qs and not giving them an inch. We led 0-3 to 0-1 after seven minutes. Diarmuid and Ciaráin Murtagh, and then Brian Stack, struck three real beauties.

In the Abbey Hotel in Roscommon town, before setting off for Hyde

Park, we had totally believed in ourselves. It was a beautiful day. There was a big crowd down from Donegal, and looking out the windows of the team bus we could feel the buzz. The pitch was in magnificent shape. The game was live on television.

Simply, it was an afternoon when it felt good to be alive.

We were able to defend alright.

The issue, the absolutely massive issue that was apparent as the first-half progressed, was that we could not get out of our own defence with the ball at all. Not enough men were willing or able to support the man on the ball.

Ultimately, we were kicking the ball long into Diarmuid Murtagh who had three or four or five Donegal defenders around him. This is how it is when you have not worked on something for six months solid.

You can hold positions.

You can block.

But you do not have a perfectly oiled transition game to move the ball out of defence with the right number of players. We did not have it. I felt sorry for Diarmuid. I also felt that I had let him down badly asking him to do the impossible.

Diarmuid Murtagh is one of the greatest forwards in the game today. He is an outstanding footballer, physically and mentally. He would enhance any team in the land. He can take chances, and he can create chances. Strong as a bull. Diarmuid Murtagh might be the greatest scoring forward in the country if he was playing for Dublin. Or some other team almost as good.

It was still tight enough coming up to half-time. Three points in it, then four. Every point counted in the final minutes of the first-half because we needed to stay alive. Go five points down, six, to a team like Donegal in the middle of the summer and you're done. I had walked into our dressing-room too many times, at half-time, knowing in my heart that the game was over. Long gone.

And as I spoke to my players on those occasions, I could see in their faces that they guessed also that the game was over.

Up one end of the field Neil McGee was giving Diarmuid Murtagh plenty of it. As far as I could see Diarmuid was getting no protection from the referee or his linesmen. And I could not get their attention.

'Stop looking at the ball!' I roared.

'Why are you looking at the action down this end?' I asked the linesman. 'Look what's happening... UP THERE!

'Off the ball... can't you see?

'Look what's happening... OFF THE BALL!'

We were not getting anyone up to help Diarmuid. But we were still not in bad shape coming up to half-time.

But... *what's with this linesman?*

The referee?

One of their kickouts did not clear the 20 metres line.

The officials didn't seem to notice.

Michael Murphy got the ball and ran at our centre-back, and drove him out of the way. A clear free out. They still don't see anything wrong. Murphy kicked the ball over the bar. Another nail in our coffin, but we were not dead. Not yet. The ball went back down the other end of the field, into Diarmuid Murtagh.

Diarmuid Murtagh is our Michael Murphy.

He should always get the benefit of the doubt in the tightest decisions.

Diarmuid won the ball. He was fouled. The referee and the linesman watched him being fouled. Nothing happened. A scuffle broke out. The referee blew the half-time whistle. Before all of this of course I'd decided to have another man-to-man talk with the linesman.

'You've got to tell the ref that he's got that wrong!

'YOU MUST...'

He told me to get out of his space.

'Move away!' he ordered. 'MOVE... AWAY!'

But I needed a free.

Murphy should have got a free against him. Murtagh should have got a free for him. We should have been three points down, not five.

I needed justice, and I could not move away. 'You're mic'ed up,' I told him. 'You have to inform the referee... tell him what you have seen.

'We're fighting for our bloody lives here!'

He shook his arm free from my hold.

The first-half was over. We were five points down. 0-10 to 0-5. Murphy had got three points in quick succession in the last seven minutes of the half. We could not get the ball out of our own half. I had to go into the dressing-room and tell my players that we were going to still win the game.

I knew we were done.

I still had to tell my players that we could win this game.

I, MORE THAN anyone, knew that we did not have the energy levels to sustain a second-half fightback against Donegal.

I know that Donegal are well able to defend.

And we could not just click out of our own defensive formation. I couldn't say... *Lads, we're going back to Plan A for the second-half!*

They'd been listening to us all week about defending. Telling them how we wanted them to defend in the largest numbers. But the part we did not place enough emphasis on, or articulate sufficiently during the week, was how were we going to get out of our own defence with the ball?

I WALKED DOWN the sideline.

The second-half was in front of me. The referee and his officials came back out.

Say nothing.

Do Nothing.

That's what I decided upon.

The linesmen had swapped sides of the field.

Good.

The man close to me was from Tipperary. Derek O'Mahony is his name, and he was standing close enough to me and there did not appear to be any big deal.

Okay... they've let it go!

The ball was about to be thrown in. But the referee did not throw the ball up. He started playing with his watch or something?

What the fuck's he doing?

'Kevin...'

The linesman had come up behind me.

'Best thing now is, Kevin,' he continued. 'I'm advising you, come out of the area and sit down... do it of your own accord.'

He was not finished talking.

'Let someone else manage the line for the second-half.'

'Why?' I asked.

He looked at me.

'No, no... it's better now if you don't make it necessary for him to come all the way across the field and have a big chat with you.

'Cameras will be on you.

'If you sit down there now, and let him throw the ball in... well, life will go on... for now.'

I knew he was right.

I turned around, and there was an empty chair positioned five yards behind me that, I presumed, belonged to a steward or someone else. I sat down on the chair. And, to his eternal credit, Seamus Sweeney, the chairman of the Roscommon county board took a second chair and sat himself down beside me. I would not be in danger of looking like a total idiot sitting there when the television cameras zoomed in on me during the second-half.

Donegal also won that half 0-10 to 0-8.

It was a 0-20 to 0-13 defeat in front of our own people.

◊ ◊ ◊ ◊ ◊

LIAM McHALE WAS my brother Paul's best friend to begin with. I ended up, I suppose, borrowing him from Paul for a good portion of the last 20 years. Liam has been by my side most of the time since 2000, when I asked him to join me on the Mayo under-21 management team, and through our years with St Brigid's and the winning of the All-Ireland club title in 2013. The two of us would have taken the Mayo senior job under our wing too, in the autumn of 2014 after James Horan resigned and I was the only person nominated for the position.

That didn't happen, of course. Twice I was the only man nominated for the Mayo job, and twice I didn't get it.

I think Liam was more disappointed than I was. We felt in our bones that we could bring another five per cent to the party and get that team over the line on which they had been stopped short for four years with James.

LIAM AND GER Dowd were my selectors for my second and third year with Roscommon. Liam has a great basketball pedigree and the complexities of that game allow him to view a football team quite differently and with greater clarity than most people. At the close of the 1980s, Liam was the best footballer in Ireland, perhaps, and he was certainly the best basketball player. Ger is a GAA man and a rugby man. He excelled in both, and he was a fabulous kicker of either ball. The rugby half of his brain was also especially valuable to me and the team, though he had preceded me as manager of St Brigid's and as much as mine or anybody else's, his handprints were on the club's All-Ireland triumph.

Ger joined us at the beginning of year two.

And Ger became my right-hand man. Ger and I would meet and talk most days. He lives just out the road from me. He replaced the legendary four-time All-Ireland winner, Mattie McDonagh as principal of Creggs National School. When he'd shut up the school for the day, I'd be waiting for him.

Ger had a good voice around the players. He was supportive, positive, but equally prepared to point out deficiencies. His presence was always reassuring but his greatest quality of all is that he is a superb human being.

Liam was our head coach, but he's always been totally unlike any stereotype of a coach. It's very hard to describe how he does what he does, but he is brilliantly effective with players. But Liam would never be seen with a flip chart or any other sort of paraphernalia. What he has is something innate. He can react on a sideline, having seen things that I have not seen.

The clarity and execution he brings has always amazed me. But equally valuable is his charisma. He's got presence, and players love working with him. One other thing, I've never heard Liam McHale say a bad word about anyone in my life. It's just his way. He rarely speaks ill of any man or woman.

Liam has a different approach to life. Basically, he loves life. He lives well, but he is not a man who needs a big car or big occasions. He likes a quiet holiday with his wife or mates. He is not extravagant in any way.

He is contented, sanguine and calmer than calm for a big man. Liam is also my brother-in-law and I was sitting with his wife, my little sister Sinéad when he was sent off early on in the 1996 All-Ireland final replay against Meath. No man deserved that shame less than Liam. I sat there, speechless, having no idea what to say to Sinéad.

Now, he's not perfect either.

AT TIMES HE has annoyed me to bits, with his approach to life. And that big-heartedness of his. A heart that was far too big for my liking in the hours after we had drawn with Mayo in the All-Ireland quarter-finals in 2017.

I was doing some after-match media duties and Liam had journeyed to the players' lounge in Croke Park to eat with the team. I've never been very much interested in eating before or after matches. But Liam likes his food. I'd been slow sorting myself out, and mainly putting everything back in some order in my brain, in the dressing-room. I said my pieces to the journalists.

I headed over, and as I entered the room I saw a clatter of Mayo bags inside the door. The Mayo crests stared back up at me.

WHAT... fuck that!

And there was Liam. Getting up from one of the tables, and shaking hands with the Mayo lads. Smiling and laughing with some of their county board men.

He saw me and sauntered over.

'Jesus Christ... Liam!'

'What's wrong?' he asked.

'What's wrong? For fuck sake, Liam... they're the same lot who kicked us up the arses when we were supposed to get the Mayo job.

'And... you're laughing and joking with them?'

I was furious.

One of the same Mayo officials had reached out his hand to me on the field after the match. And I told him to keep walking.

'I can't even bear to look at some of these people, Liam... and there you are... Chrissakes!'

I told him they were laughing at us behind our backs. Laughing their heads off at him. At me!

Liam looked flummoxed.

'What's the point?' he asked

'Why should we still be pissed off with them?'

I was too furious to reply to him. I took a minute.

'Liam... they don't mean it, when they tell you it was a great game. It's all bullshit. They just want to...

'... beat us out the gate! Do you not understand that?'

Liam did not understand me. That is the truth. The fact that someone in Croke Park had double-booked the room and allowed the two teams to sit at tables side by side, did not irritate him. If I'd known I would not have had us near them. If I'd walked into the room with our team, I would have turned us all on our heels.

'Sometimes Liam... I don't get you!'

But I do.

And two hours later I had calmed and we were back talking like brothers. That's Liam McHale. He was born, quite naturally, a good cop.

I'm the other cop because of that.

All he worries about is the players. Are they happy, is morale good? Is there a positive vibe about the place? Are we practicing well? Liam never likes to use the word training.

Training, he says, is what players do at home, when they go running around fields. They came into Roscommon sessions to practice.

Liam has always had an easy confidence about him, and the truth of it is that when I am in his company I am more confident about things working out too.

THE THREE OF us, Liam, Ger and me, we had one central philosophy about the team we wanted to build. Character came number one. Talent was a close second. Conditioning came third and that, perhaps, was our downfall in the end. But we firmly believed that if our players had character and talent, then they would make sure that they were also conditioned for what had to be done.

Let's pick fellas who'll give us everything!

That was our belief.

◊ ◊ ◊ ◊ ◊

CLOSE TO THE end of the long, hot summer of 2018 our lads had done almost everything we had asked of them.

Get back into Division One of the league?

Box ticked.

Retain our Connacht title?

Empty box.

Win our way through to the Super 8s?

Box ticked.

It would have been a magical piece of history if Roscommon had claimed two Connacht titles back-to-back, but we definitely gave it our best shot.

Everybody was mostly happy. The county board were very happy. The players knew that they had made it through to the last eight, and were getting to play alongside the best teams in the country in the newly fangled and big branded Super 8s.

'Jaysus, Mayo have never been in the Super 8s!' one supporter shouted into my ear after we had beaten Armagh to make it through.

We had all made one county extremely happy. I was possibly the only person in the place who was regretful. We should have beaten Galway in the Connacht final. It was a big regret.

It would have meant... EVERYTHING!

For the people of Roscommon to defeat Galway in two finals in quick succession would have been enormous.

For the team, it would have stabilised everything and something more.

It would have LAUNCHED us.

THE MOMENT IN 2018 when I knew we were now in the biggest trouble?

It hit me in Tullamore.

July 7. We had beaten Armagh 2-22 to 1-19 in round four of the qualifiers. There was one point in it with the game about done. But we closed out stronger than them. We got the crucial late points. And we got a second goal from Enda Smith.

We were on our way home from Portlaoise in our beautiful team bus that had been kitted out to make the Roscommon football team look, like any professional team you might see in any country in Europe, a prized outfit.

The bus has a table in the centre for the management to sit facing one another, and chat and work things out on laptop and paper if they need to. Liam was sitting opposite me.

Ger had stayed back in Portlaoise to watch Cork and Tyrone play. The winner would be in our four-team group in the Super 8s, but I didn't need to see it. I'd have the match served up to me digitally. Besides, it had been a scorcher of a day. under the stand, locked up in the dressing-room in O'Moore Park, it was outrageously warm. It was overpowering.

It caused us problems before the match, and again at half-time. We needed to get our lads home, and let them hydrate and ice down and basically rest their bones. Also, I had no sense that Cork would put it up to Tyrone.

We had played them in a challenge game in Portlaoise, on a back pitch two weeks earlier, and we had run through them. We took the game against Cork just to buzz ourselves up. We knew we were playing well despite losing to Galway in the Connacht final. It was a Wednesday evening. A magnificent summer's evening. We always took our challenge matches very seriously, because we took on so few of them.

Challenge is the wrong name for them.

There is no such thing as a challenge match in the GAA at the highest level any longer. Every game is a serious piece of business.

We were brilliant. We tore Cork apart.

Ohhhh GEEEEEEE.

Were we bubbling as a team?

YESSSSSSS.

The game against Armagh had become a shootout. Pure and simple, the two teams went out there like two primed heavyweights and both of us threw every punch we had ever locked away. It was brave and honest football.

I loved every second of it. It didn't start out like that but that is how it ended. Maybe it was the heat. Maybe it fried our brains.

Though I knew that other managers watching, those who got to look at it on their TV screens and dissect it, would sit back and smile to themselves. And label the game ridiculous. And Kieran McGeeney and myself?

Fools, most probably, would be the consensus.

Because neither of us had our defences loaded when it mattered most.

Neither of us even swept all that much in the end. Kieran and myself just wanted to see which team had the stronger chin.

True.

We did.

AT THE FINAL whistle, I had felt a huge relief. Everything we had promised ourselves, and our county board and our supporters and our sponsors at the start of the year, was done. Promotion to Division One. A spot in the Super 8s. A gutsy defence of our Connacht title in between. And the FBD title thrown in as an early season bonus.

Then Tullamore.

We'd talked through the win over Armagh before arriving at the town, and soaked up the different things that had worked out brilliantly, moves... individual players... and then we hit Tullamore for our team meal. There was a lull in the conversation.

I was thinking.

Recovery tomorrow.

Session Tuesday. Who's injured...

Who'll need another week to get back?

Tyrone....

When will I get to see the Tyrone game?

Ger would have his update on Tyrone. But Liam and I would be waiting for the game to be available in the digital library which is presented to every management team through their personal PIN access. A whole different world to when I was a footballer. A digital library, and also teams sharing stats from games. Well, most of the teams. Some of the big boys don't like to share.

Kerry? No interest in sharing anything.

'OH LIAM...

'WE'RE SO UP AGAINST IT...

'WE'RE IN SUCH TROUBLE!'

That's what I heard coming out of my mouth.

It was a dawning moment.

THERE WAS NO denying it. I could close my eyes and see it. Tyrone were built to play in the Super 8s. Three games in four weeks and nowhere to hide. Tyrone were ready for that.

We were not ready for anything more.

That's what I understood as we left Tullamore behind us. We were not ready for Tyrone. They had better conditioning than us. Unlike us, they had been built up over a number of years, brick by brick, until Mickey Harte had the seamless interaction of a 28-man squad, and they also had a mental hardness that we did not possess. They had other advantages. They had a process.

Yes, that horrible word. Tyrone had a process about mostly everything they did out there. Every time we played them there was always a sense of foreboding. I'd watch them go... and go and go. I knew they would take us out of it, and that it was only a matter of time.

With Tyrone, when you see a big player going off their team there is no sense of relief. He may be a player we had scouted and taken care of particularly before the game. But the player running onto the field to replace him will look no different. He'll look as strong and as athletic, and just as deathly serious.

Tyrone also had the most finely tuned hand-passing. Their hand-passing and support play looked magnificent and appeared effortless. Tyrone had it all, apart from their finishing which was not as good as the very top teams. They miss a lot for the amount of ball they get. And a lot of it is careless auld misses. Brilliant players you wouldn't expect to miss.

But they do.

The importance of expert hand-passing in the modern game, however, is the key to so much. Tyrone will not put the ball a yard too far in front of the man looking, or half a yard behind him. He'll not have to check. Tyrone will not put the ball at the man's knees. They'll not make the man reach over his head for the ball.

I CONTINUALLY TOLD my own players.

'Give the pass so that the receiver makes the decision...

'... don't give the pass so you have made the decision for him!'

A BAD PASS, and you have made the decision for him. There's a goal chance lost, or a breakout of defence is slowed down. Tyrone are not the best team in Ireland at hand-passing. That is still Kerry.

Kerry boys are brought up to be the most natural ball players in the whole country. It's bred into them, and then coached. But after three years with the Roscommon lads there were still too many casual passes.

A pass thrown out of our defence.

Or a pass lazily fisted sideways as we reached the outer line of the opposing defence. A pass that made our man stretch for it, that took him half a second to bring the ball in or bring the ball down. That vital, tiniest split of a second. Our receiving man had lost the slim advantage that had been there. The next pass he has to make is already compromised. The action is tight around him. He is going into heavy traffic. He had to win the ball. He had to protect himself and the ball.

All because of one sloppy pass.

Casual, lazy, sloppy passing. The death of every team wanting to be as good as Kerry and Tyrone, and Mayo, and Donegal on a very good day.

WE WERE DRIVING home from Portlaoise, and I knew in my heart that we did not have the solid defensive core that Tyrone would have, then Donegal, and finally Dublin in our group.

Neither did we have the power or the size to break down their defensive lines.

The excitement of beating Armagh had gone.

Portlaoise was history.

Croke Park is a faster pitch. It's lightning. Seven days, and the wild shootout against Armagh would mean nothing. Actually, it had damaged us. We were less prepared than ever for a game of football that would be played as though it was thought up by mathematicians and scientists.

Mickey Harte might aswell be wearing a white coat himself when his players come into him. He knows they will arrive conditioned, that they will be in the best possible physical shape. That gives him all the time he needs to work out what he wants to do with them with the highest level of practice.

He'll have Colm Cavanagh dropping back

He'll have players repeatedly breaking off the arrowhead they apply when coming out of their defence. Tiernan McCann will be over-lapping and over-lapping... lapping for Ireland. We'd nobody like him.

Roscommon have some of the most skilful footballers in Ireland, massive skill levels. But we had no size. We had limited conditioning. We had only so much power, and not enough for 70 minutes and some minutes more out on Croke Park's zippy surface which appears tailor-made for men and women with Olympic qualifying times and achievements behind them.

That's the problem with skilful players.

It's been the big issue in Roscommon for as long as I have lived in the county, which is now almost 30 years. Skilful players, when they're teenagers and younger men never have to work hard enough on the physical side of their game.

Their skills serve them as a lottery ticket for far too long in their own neck of the woods. And when they reach manhood and have to prove themselves in the big, bad world, well, unfortunately, they do not have that physique or that level of conditioning to allow them to succeed. They just don't have it in the bank.

I'M NOT TALKING about all the Roscommon players.

We had six, maybe seven lads who had prepared and had done the long and hard physical shifts for years and years. They were ready for the high altitude football that was the Super 8s. The others? They'd knuckled down for the three years, for us. Because we'd asked them.

And some had knuckled down better than others.

Two-thirds of the Roscommon squad was not ready for the Super 8s. All those individuals had not done the four or five years of deep conditioning necessary.

They hadn't the bulk.

And they hadn't the aerobic qualification to do what had to be done.

I can hardly believe I am writing that, but I just have!

Aerobic qualification!

◊ ◊ ◊ ◊ ◊

MY SISTERS TELL me that Verona is the World's greatest listener.

Verona is my wife.

She is also a psychologist.

Us football and hurling managers, we have our heads full of plans, and dreams and hopes, most of them dashed or about to hit a wall, and we also have our theories. About other managers and teams, and about our own players. We have a lot going on in our heads.

It's got to be a help to have your wife holding down such a job, right? I guess it is, and for starters her 'problems' put mine as a football manager into sharp perspective. I had retired from the army, and I was giving the Roscommon job every hour that it needed.

We all want to have our opinions out there, but Verona will sit there and listen, and she will weigh up the situation. In her daily work, however, she is dealing with real life, and really tough situations. She is an educational psychologist, and working with parents who might be devastated by the challenges their child is facing. Me winning or losing a football match by a point does not add up to a hill of beans compared to Verona's working life, but she knows it is big in my life.

She recognises my moods and makes allowances for them.

I share everything with her, but she is not watching me, or observing me. And my excessive emotions are not entering a secret diary by her bedside.

But she will see me coming in from training, and hear me talking to myself. Or I might be getting ready for a match and I will be throwing things out there. I might be saying what I am going to do with someone who is a serious problem for me... and Verona will look at me, and quietly say...

'What's wrong?'

I might tell her that the individual in question did not show at training. Actually went missing, with no warning, no phone call... high treason!

'Come on now,' she might say. 'Maybe there's a good reason.

'Maybe he lost his job.

'Maybe he had a problem he could not talk to you about... don't dive in and have to apologise to him later, because someone in his family died.'

She helps me calm.

And she makes good suggestions, but I often wonder have I enough common sense as a football manager to actually listen to her at times and take her advice?

VERONA PLAYED A massive role in raising our children.

I have never been around as often as I should, through football, and because of my army life. I served in a lot of places away from home. I lived in different barracks from Monday to Friday. I did three tours overseas for six months at a time on each occasion. And I managed six football teams, before I became manager of Roscommon. There were long tranches when I was simply not here.

I met Verona Cope when she was a month shy of her 17th birthday.

Her father, Howard was a dentist from Birmingham who came to the west of Ireland, to Ballina to his wife, Vera's home town. I was 20 and a cadet in the army. Sweet Jesus, even now I wonder how her parents got their heads around that? Their beautiful daughter. And me?

We met because of Kenneth Hanley, who was a cadet in the army with me. We were both from Ballina and travelled home together from The Curragh. Kenneth and I, we had this three weeks of an army adventure training module based out of Castlebar, learning to absail and climb mountains, and sleep on the side of a mountain.

Kenneth and I were commissioned in April, 1984 as officers. We were commissioned on a Monday. On the Thursday Kenneth had an horrific car accident and never served another day in the army.

But Kenneth was the reason why I met my wife. He got an invite to a lad's 21st birthday party. It read... 'Peter invites Kenneth...' but when I was finished with the same card it read... 'Peter invites Kenneth... and Kevin.' The officer who looked at the invite signed it off. In Ballina rugby club I met my future wife and saviour.

We were married in Arbour Hill and had our reception in Collins Barracks in Dublin in 1991. Emma, our first daughter, was born two years later. I was practically going out the door to Lebanon on my first tour when we got the news about that pregnancy. I was six and a half months out there, with only one trip home. It was a tough pregnancy and mid-term there was an issue and Verona was confined to bed.

The twins, Caoimhe and Megan were born in 1997, about one minute apart. Verona had to raise our family, not single-handedly, but she had to use both hands too often. Meanwhile, I was doing things I loved doing.

LOOKING BACK NOW, I see how unfair I was.

I had my career in the military. I was managing football teams, I was working all hours at weekends as a commentator and analyst for RTE.

My life has flown by.

I took on too much. I trained Roscommon Gaels here in the town while I was working and living midweek in Dublin. The madness of it now genuinely shocks me. Crazy, but luckily we won the senior championship. But it was still an insane act. On more than one occasion I drove down from Dublin in the early evening to take a training session and got right back into my car and hightailed it back to Dublin because I had work to do for the following morning. I did not even have time to call into my own home to say hello to my wife and girls.

Verona said she always understood.

It gets to the stage where some of us put our football life before things that are really far more important. I was guilty of that. But you can't step back. You have made a commitment. The next game seriously looks like something that is a matter of life and death, or thereabouts. It became an obsession for me.

Verona, meanwhile, kept all the balances in our home.

Our girls are amazing young women. And that is down to their mother, and also Verona's mother and father, who moved to live close to us, and helped to pick up the pieces while I was racing around football grounds.

WHEN MY TIME with Roscommon came to an end and my health was beginning to be questioned, and the stress levels were ridiculously high, Verona and I finally had long conversations. We went for walks and chatted.

'Do we need to do this?'

'Is it time to have a bit more time for us?'

I had given it three full, jam-packed years with Roscommon, and 20 years managing other teams before that. Verona and I decided that it was time to retire for good as a football manager.

And, here's the mad bit.

If there was a knock on the door tomorrow or the telephone rang, and the man on the other end asked if I was interested in taking the Mayo job, what would I say?

I'd tell him yes, and I'd spend the next few hours getting up the nerve to explain to Verona why they need me, and why I need them, and that I simply have to be the next Mayo football manager.

◊ ◊ ◊ ◊ ◊

OVER A PERIOD of two and a half years, Roscommon had the highest scoring percentages from play in the country. We were up at 83 per cent at one point.

We needed to be right up there, because we were not winning enough frees.

Open play was our life blood.

Normally, most football teams have over 30 per cent plus of their scores coming from free-kicks.

But not us.

FREES ARE A result of forward pressure.

A man runs hard at a defensive line, and he gets fouled. The free-taker taps it over. That is the punishment for fouling a powerful runner. Your expert free-taker gets a relatively easy shot at goal with nobody within 10 yards of him. He can take all the time in the world.

Roscommon did not have power.

We did not have very many direct line runners at all. We had lovely fluid movement down the field, but we could not physically engage the very top teams and force them to foul.

Not getting those frees was a serious deficiency.

They're the easy ones!

The two Murtaghs, Diarmuid and Ciaráin, they are brilliant free-takers. Diarmuid would be able to shoot it out with Dean Rock or Cillian O'Connor, the sharpest boots in the land. Ciaráin would not be far behind them. Those are the frees that keep you alive, keep you within two or three points of the very best teams. But we were not getting those free-kicks.

So, from play, we had to be scoring practically everything to have half a chance. And we had to do so against a Tyrone defence that always had nine, 10 or 11 men manning the barricades. And Tyrone do pressure better than anybody.

A one-on-one between one of our forwards and one of their defenders was going to be a rarity. One against two defenders, and we'd be lucky. I knew that.

But those two Tyrone defenders would have a third man close at hand and one of them would be able to get a block in.

They would never stop pressurising. Hassling, tackling and blocking. It's hard to score against that type of defence, it's actually hard to breathe.

UNLESS YOU ARE Dublin.

Seventy per cent of Dublin's shooting at goal in the 2018 All-Ireland final was uncontested. Dublin, amazingly, were playing Tyrone and still they were able to manufacture shots at goal where there was no Tyrone defender in sight practically.

Dublin will rarely try to shoot when they have a man left unmarked, and uncontested. They are so patient. Also, they do not have too many men capable of shooting points from long range. Only Diarmuid Connolly and Dean Rock are able to put them over from 40 metres out or more.

The others? Paul Flynn was always erratic under pressure. Paddy Andrews and Kevin McManamon are no better. Same with Ciaran Kilkenny. With nobody near his boot he will kick them over all day from 30 metres out. Same with Brian Fenton. Dublin move the ball and keep it moving, shifting over and back across the field, like counting up the phases in a game of rugby, until...until they have a man in space, or until they have someone coming in at speed and getting on to the end of a pass and forcing a free within the 45 metres line.

Dublin can wait until a defender falls off a tackle or another defender just falls asleep watching the ball switch back and forth in front of his eyes.

I KNEW WE would not get any easy scoring chances against Tyrone.

And when Mickey Harte and his helpers were finished their homework, I knew that Diarmuid Murtagh would have several circles in red and black pen around his name. Enda Smith too. Enda was capable of causing Tyrone trouble with his brilliant running from deep.

He'd also be circled on paper, and circled out on the field.

Enda is exceptional at carrying the ball forward, but falling back into defence is not his strength. He is no Colm Cavanagh. He does not have a massive aerobic ability. The best man we had to counter the likes of Colm Cavanagh and utilise him deeper in our half of the field was young Tadhg O'Rourke. But Tadhg was still a rookie. He is a magnificent physical specimen of a young man, but he had lots to learn, and we could not use him to sweep in front of our full-back line. We needed Tadhg in the middle of the field.

We had to have some strength and mobility in the middle third.

We didn't have much strength in depth. Before I got the job, John Evans had led Roscommon from Division Four, to Division Three, to Division Two, to Division One. It was a brilliant achievement. But all of the Roscommon lads had spent their whole careers in the lower divisions, and down there you get away with things. There might be four lads on the other team with massive ability, but the other 11? They'll be off the pace to different degrees.

You can avoid being found out in the lower divisions.

AND THEN THERE was me.

I have to put my hand up. It was never my natural inclination to set up defensively. And once we reached the Super 8s I knew we were banjaxed. I knew we hadn't got the physicality to compete. The players knew we hadn't got the system to compete. I could see them looking at me. I could read their thoughts.

We can't compete here!

There was something else about the Roscommon lads. They never liked enough contact. Not everyone, but as a collective the lads in the dressing-room were not hard enough or rough enough in how we went about our business.

They did not bring that cutting edge to their tackling.

They didn't feed off overturns.

It's not in the nature of this Roscommon team.

Of course, we had our defined method of defending. Like every team I managed, we had a matched-up zone where there were certain opposing players with higher abilities who were receiving specialised attention. Like everyone else, we believed in and operated a 'Weak Side' defence.

If the opposition are carrying the ball down one side of our defence, then our corner and half-back on the other side will drift towards the centre. There is no point in them staying in their positions when the ball is coming down the far side. There is seldom any question of the ball being lashed diagonally across the field anymore.

That's how the smart teams play.

Nos.3 and 6 stay central. An aerobic midfielder is also back there, in the mix, doing his thing. So, you have a narrow set-up of six defenders playing 'Weak Side', you have Nos.10 and 12 topping the zone, and No.8 back in there. It's all basic enough. The whole idea is to put bodies in the way of shots.

Nobody pushes out dramatically when the other team reach the 45 metres line. If the other team think they can score from there, then we can live with that. But other teams don't risk scores from outside the 45 metres line anymore.

If you have a turnover, then you also have bodies breaking out of defence. If you can get the ball on the first pass to your best or most imaginative player, then he will have bodies either side of him moving up the field.

He will have runners, and it is up to him to find them.

That's the simplicity of 'Weak Side' defence.

All the smartest and best teams play like this.

It is how I set up the Mayo under-21s for four years. It is how I set up all the club teams I managed, including St Brigid's when we won the All-Ireland title.

That's how it was with Roscommon.

But, when the ball came inside the 45 metres line, we didn't have what the very best teams in the country have, we did not make enough of a... Bang!

Bang!

Bang, bang... BANG!

Our lads were not good at putting in the biggest hits. It didn't come naturally to them. Simply, it was not in their nature.

NOT LIKE MAYO.

We all know that any time you get a man inside the Mayo 45 metres line there is the gravest danger of him being stripped of the ball.

Every tackle they make is hard.

The first hit shakes the man with the ball.

The next hit shakes him up more and, as the man seeks to balance himself and regain some composure, regain some sense of what he has to do... they'll probably have stripped him of possession. Mayo at their best are the best team in the country at stripping ball.

They are brilliant at it. Even in one-on-one situations a Mayo defender backs himself to win the ball back. In the 2017 All-Ireland final against Dublin, Chris Barrett did it four times in the second-half. Each time in a one-on-one situation. It was an amazing example of pressurised, physical, half-crazed, but composed defending.

Mayo love that.

They love to see someone strip the ball, and when they drive out of defence they do so with a real sense of triumph and imminent threat.

Mayo are the No.1 tacklers.

Tyrone, however, are No.1 in minding their defence.

MAYO, OF COURSE, were not always natural tacklers.

The Mayo psyche, a bit like Roscommon, and also Galway, is to get the ball and play ball.

It is a deep rooted thing in the game in all three counties, and it remains one of the biggest difficulties for Galway as they attempt to reach the level of competitiveness that Mayo reached for most of the last decade.

I was also very conscious of this from day one with Roscommon. I had been at so many Roscommon games as a spectator, as Hyde Park is 200 metres from my front door. I'd see them playing, and they might have 14 men behind the ball.

Some of those games might be level at half-time, but it had been horrendous to watch for all of us in the stand. You'd overhear someone down from you say to a pal... 'It's not too bad... we're level with them!'

But, nearly every time against the top teams, the whole Roscommon performance would soon cave in after that, and they would lose by six or seven points. And the same supporters would be grumbling as they shuffled to the gates.

When I took the job, a great number of my Roscommon football friends said to me... 'Let's play ball!' They did not have to say it to me a second time.

I wanted Roscommon to play football.

Maybe I was naive. But that is how I made my bed.

◊ ◊ ◊ ◊ ◊

HARD WORK NEVER worried me.

Nor did it worry the Kevin McStay who came before me. I have this memory or idea of my father killing himself working, until he could work no more. My mother and father were both from Tuam, but they met in Ballina and fell in love on their shared journeys home at weekends. My mother was one of 12 Holians. My father was one of four children, and was working in the post office in Ballina when Maidie Holian arrived into town as a 16 years-old girl ready to take up work in Clarke's newsagents. Our first house in the town was in Marian Crescent, right bang in the middle of things, but there was soon a big family of McStays on the way. My mother explains, in her true style, that she had a 'lot of love to give' and she did so, to...

Mary.

Sandra.

Rory.

Linda.

Me.

Paul.

Gráinne,

Fiona.

Brian.

Sinéad.

And Laura.

There was also my uncle Noel, who was one of my great mentors in life, who came and lived with us for a period of time as he was working locally.

Halfway through it was necessary to move from the Crescent. My father said he got lucky with money once in his life and, after a friend of his had encouraged him to buy shares in Tynagh Mines, he was able to cash out and he bought and built on a site in Kilmore just outside of the town.

The work ethic in our home was strong, and I was making my own money for as long as I can remember. I guess from 10 years of age I worked in every fourth or fifth shop on Ballina's Main Street at different times. I must have worked in 15 different shops. I was also a newspaper boy, and a messenger boy and telegram boy.

I'd get the old *Evening Press* and the *Evening Herald*, usually about 20 of each and I'd get them sold. I was outside mass with the Sunday newspapers, too.

On a Thursday lunchtime my father would get his weekly wage. It would be contained in a small green envelope that normally housed telegrams, and it would be in cash, with an elastic band around it. My mother would be waiting for it.

And I was the expert messenger boy, of course.

I'd cycle up to the post office to get the wages and I would push the packet as deep as I could into my pocket. Lose that green envelope and, I knew, I may aswell keep on cycling and not stop when I hit Athlone.

EDUCATION WAS SOMETHING my mother truly believed in.

She had had a great life and she enjoyed her life. This showed when she was on the dancefloor especially. Maidie McStay was a champion dancer. She was a Connacht waltzing champion at one point, though not with my father, who did not have two steps. Uncle Paddy was her partner.

My mother worked hard all her life. She had set out for London, at one point, at 17 years of age, and spent a year working in Euston Station in the middle of the city. Herself and my father never spent much money on themselves once they had a family. He would like an occasional drink with his friends up the town. But that petered out when there were more of us around the family table.

His back garden was so large and ample that, once we had our fill of the scallions and lettuce, the rhubarb, the onions and potatoes, he'd have enough left over to regularly supply Fahy's, our local grocery store.

They needed the extra money. While my mother was a fabulous cook, she also needed to be industrial about her kitchen methods because breakfasts and lunchtimes, dinner time, these were big events in the McStay house. Mostly, the hard work was aimed at good education for us. Mary, Sandra, Rory and Linda, from the first half of our family for instance, all were sent to full boarding school. Paul and myself went as day boys to St Jarlath's, when we lived with our aunts in Tuam.

I WAS LUCKY.

I had an incredibly happy childhood, and was a part of a great family. I was blessed. And I found it hard leaving home. I found it hard leaving for Jarlath's, and I found it even harder leaving for the army when I was about to be locked away effectively in a barracks in The Curragh for 18 months.

'There is nothing here for you, Kevin!' I can still remember my mother telling me. 'You have to make your life happen!'

I loved Ballina.

My town. Going to the bog or the woods, under orders from my father, and doing my own things. I lived in a bubble that was filled with the woods and fishing, working my jobs, and trying to win at everything. Soccer, football, squash, tennis, snooker, basketball... I would have been happy to stay in Ballina and stay a young man forever.

I WAS BUILT into the man I am today by a number of amazing people. My father for one. My national school teacher, Tom Maughan. Like my father, Tom is one of my great heroes. Big Tom, to us. He led me from 12 to 14 years of age through life, and through my earliest football fields.

Tom Maughan kept it real. No messing. He'd been a goalkeeper with Mayo. He was good friends with my father, but it was Tom who brought me to my first Connacht final. In Scoil Padraig, Tom had us believing we were playing serious football. We were flying it, and we won the North Mayo title every single year.

In the street league in town, Gerry Kenny, a fantastic footballer and soccer player, organised us. We were St Pat's and we wore a Galway coloured jersey. It was Gerry who showed me how to play as a corner-forward. I was off to a good start in my football education. I had Tom when I was on the Ballina Stephenites under-14s, and Terry Reilly, the editor of the *Western People* newspaper, at under-16s. We won the under-14 county title. I was 13 and captained the team the next year to another one. We won three under-16 titles. Then we won a minor title, and an under-21 title.

But it all began with Tom Maughan, who had us as a captive audience. Tom also had a trick up his sleeve which he called his Seventh Class.

I think he thought it up for boys who might be struggling that little bit and could do with an extra year. But then he extended this idea. The best footballers were encouraged to do Seventh Class, and I did, going back in September and taking my place in a row of seats just to the left of the main class that contained five or six other lads, nearly all of them the school's best footballers.

I had a complete football education. It was Terry Reilly who raised the stakes, seeing to it that tackling was a bit harder and dressing-room talks were a bit keener. Up to then it was all about the craic and winning. Terry loved us hand-passing. He had oil barrels and we'd have to hand-pass the ball into them to score a goal. We could hand-pass like Tyrone and Kerry hand-pass today!

With basketball huge in the town, nearly everyone on the team had lovely, soft hands. Terry was also into making space, three-man midfields and two-man full-forward lines. Terry was ahead of his time, and I was the man spreading the word on his behalf, his messenger boy.

I'd head off on my bike with a bunch of postcards on which he had written his orders for the week for training. Why not, I was also Terry Reilly's newspaper boy hitting houses on my bike aswell. There was Tom and Terry, and my Dad, and Willie Casey, an iconic Mayo footballer who was over us at minor and more traditional in his thinking than Terry.

Willie was not mad about all this hand-passing. Whereas Terry would have nothing high going into the full-forward line, not a single stray ball, Willie wanted a big lad in there and he wanted a little lad like me to play off him when the ball was lashed in, early and high.

Willie thought of football as fun. Terry thought it more of a serious business. Together, with the pair of them and so many other hard working men, we were made to feel the cream of Mayo football.

WE WERE TOLD we were the Stephenites.

We were told that we were born to be winners. Born to play for Mayo.

But Ballina Stephenites had not won a Mayo senior title since 1966. The club had more senior titles than all of the other clubs in the county added together, apart from Castlebar Mitchells, but the town was waiting.

The wait would continue for me and the Stephenites for five long perishing years until, finally, with Noel O'Dowd from Lanesboro and Willie Casey, and Niall Heffernan and Padhraic Lynn, we did it in 1985. I was captain two years later when we won the title again.

We played Castlebar in the final, in Ballina. It was like Real Madrid and Barcelona going to war on a fabulous warm afternoon in our own field. Castlebar had taken the title back from us in 1986. In '87 Liam McHale scored a goal and a point. My brother, Paul took a point. I put one over the bar. Martin Carney kicked two points for them. There were three points in it at the finish.

1-8 to 2-2.

IN MY FINAL year in St Jarlath's I had no football to play. I was overage. Sounds incredible, but true. After I finished up in Scoil Padraig at 13 years of age, I attended St Muredach's in Ballina and also the Vocational School, before heading to Jarlath's. Three different secondary schools.

Muredach's did not seem to have a care in the world about football. I spent half a year there and I found it awful. I left after being pummelled by one teacher in the classroom, simply for looking at him the wrong way, I guess in his estimation, after he had given another boy in the class a couple of serious clips.

I was a small 13 year old, and he gave me an awful battering. I was hit on the body and the head repeatedly. He then threw me out of the classroom. I was a bloodied mess cycling home.

It was late March. I never went back to Muredach's, though my father did have an unsolicited meeting with the teacher in question, and the following

September myself and Paul started first year together in Ballina Vocational School, where we both had the time of our lives with outstanding teachers. But for our Leaving Cert, Mum and Dad sent us to St Jarlath's. In Tuam, I lived with my Auntie Eileen and Uncle Michael, where I was part of the family, right down to receiving my pocket money from them on Fridays. Daithí Quinn, another big influence in my youth, had taught me in Ballina but had now got a job in St Jarlath's, so I was very comfortable in my new environment.

Football coursed through the veins at Jarlath's which is one of the legendary homes of football in the west. Me and Jarlath's was a marriage made in Heaven. We had morning study and evening study, and we also had football every single day. But, then, like a guillotine fast at work, I was separated from everything to do with football in my final year there. I was overage. My circuitous journey through my three secondary schools left me out of the loop.

I WAS SOON in the mood to drift through life.

People who don't know me seem to think I have a grand plan about my life, but I don't, and never had. I am someone who tumbles along.

I was certainly tumbling through my late teenage years. I was looked on as one of the best on the Mayo minor team, and I should have gone straight onto the under-21s, but I could not have been bothered. I went to the RTC in Galway to study construction. I was hit and miss there. I passed my exams, barely, and left after one year. I also fell out of love with football for a period. I played championship with the Stephenites, but only because I had no choice.

Other than that, there was no convincing reason in my head to put football before having a good time. I learned to drink in the RTC. I fluted around. I knew I was drifting, and I was happy enough about that.

It was only when I joined the army in late 1982 that I reconnected with my old life, and the ball.

◊ ◊ ◊ ◊ ◊

THE SECOND-HALF of our Super 8s match against Tyrone was a true heart-breaker.

It was a killer to watch from the sideline, though team managers are the perennial optimists. We suffered a very public humiliation against Tyrone in Croke Park in our first game in the Super 8s. As one manager before me once explained, not fussed about too much eloquence, it was... 'like having your guts ripped out'.

No anaesthetic either.

I stood and I sat.

I sat for 30 seconds, and then I was back on my feet again.

I knew I had to do something, but it was total damage limitation. Winning the game was out of the question by half-time.

My haunting memory of too many games against the biggest and best teams in my three years with Roscommon is one of walking into our dressing-room at half-time, to talk to my players, knowing that the game was long over. Winning the second-half was all that we could try to do against Tyrone. We were in the Super 8s and the GAA's newly branded finale to the championship was full of primed teams.

We were not one of them.

Winning the second-half would be harder than winning the first-half.

My pride, at the same time, was on the floor and being trod upon. I was conscious of all the people from Roscommon who had driven up to Dublin for a day full of excitement, and some hope of a result. I was aware of all the people back home in the county watching the game live on television.

The second 35 minutes of our opening game in the Super 8s was car crash TV.

I was in charge of the crash.

I KNEW EVERYONE would be extremely tough in their judgment of us. I could live with that. That was always okay with me, once it was fair and reasonable.

It's a central part of what you sign up for when you accept the job of managing a county. I knew what they would be thinking in the press box and the broadcasting boxes up in the Hogan Stand.

I had spent almost 20 years up there with them.

Talking amongst ourselves.

Individually arriving at big conclusions.

I was down on the sideline, which is a noisy place to be at any time in Croke Park, but I could hear them.

'The naivety of them....

'... coming up here to Croker... and trying to play like that!

'Against Tyrone!'

As a writer and a commentator, you are not actually living the game.

As a manager, you're alive within the same game.

As a manager, you know exactly what is happening, and why!

As a writer and commentator, you can arrive at all-encompassing, bland statements and you can dole them out without a worry in the world about being backed-up.

'Arrag... they're not up to it!'

'The innocence of them... they haven't a clue!'

WE STOOD OUTSIDE the dressing-room, and listened to what David Joyce, the team's strength and conditioning coach, had to say at half-time during the Tyrone game.

He told us that three of our lads were 'gassed out'.

David said they were gone.

They needed to be subbed.

This was something I also had to live with during my three years with Roscommon. We never had enough brilliantly conditioned players who could go the whole way out to 55 minutes, maybe 60 minutes, at full throttle. Some of our players were finished after 35 minutes.

Whether it was injuries, or simply not having enough in the tank, but we found ourselves compromised in our selections and in our needs at half-time. Too many of our best footballers, once they had done everything we asked of them from the first minute, dropping back into a 'Weak Side' defence, getting back up the field, contesting in the middle third... too many were sucking for air at half-time.

David told us a second time that three of our lads were finished.

They've nothing left in them, he insisted.

I knew he was right.

Liam and Ger and myself, we always told the lads that they had to empty the tank. We told them they could not hedge their bets. They could not wait for a big final 20 minutes.

This was a big thing for us as a management team.

The three of us knew that everything was different to our own playing days, when we'd all have the final quarter on our minds, all of us regularly enough slicing up the parts of the game when you'd go full out, and when you'd hold that little bit back. The modern game of football is a more honest game.

Our Roscommon team, by the late summer of 2018, was an honest team.

TYRONE WERE NINE points up.

Or 10, maybe.

I had stopped looking up at the scoreboard.

But then I'd look up at the scoreboard, and see they were actually 12 points ahead of us.

Jaysus... there's still 25 minutes left!

ENDA SMITH GOT a great goal. And Ciaráin Murtagh got through for another goal. It was back to a five points game, five or six points?

This isn't over...

Not yet... we might...

FUCK. FUCK... IT!

In the final quarter, as David Joyce had told us, warned us, made doubly sure we knew even though he also knew we could not act on all of his advice, the floodgates were opened again.

Too many yellow shirts were not moving, not moving fast enough. Or hard enough. There were no more big tackles from us.

To begin with, we didn't have a defensive structure fit for Tyrone. By the end, how could we expect it to be any different.

ON THE BUS, on the way home from the Tyrone battering, I already had the next game filling up my head. Donegal, and game two in the Super 8s.

Donegal!

The Hyde!
One week... Saturday!

◊ ◊ ◊ ◊ ◊

ONE OF THE best decisions I made in my life was joining the army, and one of the best decisions I made was to leave the army.

The army made me. Certainly, it finished off the excellent work that so many good people in my life had begun. From a young age, I had thought of becoming a teacher, but I never did enough to get there.

Too much time was spent dreaming. I'm a dreamer by nature. My mother suggested the army to me. On November 29, 1982, I was in, which was no mean feat as there were huge numbers vying for cadetships. Thirty-two years later, I was out.

It began in Cadet School in The Curragh, where I spent 18 months and where it was the army's business to straighten out my head. There was no dreaming for those 18 months. They were torturous most of the time. Great, but definitely torturous. And not always so great either.

Overnight, I was owned.

Up at 6.15 in the mornings, and lucky to get back into my bed by 11.0 that night. We had no idea when, or if, we'd ever get home. Every day took a physical toll. There was the constant training, and there was also the academic side, and at the end of it I got to go back to college, to UCG, which was a fine prize for everyone, and which for someone like me, from a huge family, was an extra fattened prize. Of course, I got to UCG and mostly messed up my opportunity there.

Slobbering, as my father might have put it.

Fluting around and dreaming.

I spent three years in UCG studying for my engineering degree, but after being locked up for 18 months, I was also out of control. I was dreadful. I let myself down. I was playing Collingwood soccer and Sigerson football, and basketball. I was playing snooker, and drinking. I was doing everything and I was doing nothing very well. I never applied myself, and didn't qualify, and two decades would pass before I made up for that... that slobbering, and stood in full military uniform, my wife on one side of me, my mother on the other, with a Masters.

FOR THOSE 18 months, we always seemed to be carrying some load or other. A rifle and a pack, or some other load. Every day, we were owned by someone. Even when you got home, you were still army property. You had to leave the barracks in a blazer. I'd feel an arrow pointed straight down at my tight shaved head, as I sat on the train home to Ballina.

Before heading anywhere near the train station, you'd have to parade. And if you were not spotless, then you were not getting on any train. You would be presented with another 24 hours to turn out spotless.

AS THE ARMY was going about its business of straightening me out, it was no surprise really that I became one of the best footballers in Mayo. I won an Allstar award within three years.

Typically, I was sitting on a chair getting my head shaved, which was a fortnightly ritual in The Curragh, when the barber told me to pick up a copy of the paper to one side. It was the *Evening Press*.

'Is that you?' he asked. 'It's you... isn't it!'

BIG SURPRISE AS McSTAY SELECTED FOR MAYO

There were no phones in sight very much in the early 80s.

There was no letter sent to me to say I'd been selected on the Mayo team for the Connacht final in 1983. I had never trained with the team. Though Liam O'Neill knew about me and he wanted someone who could shoot the lights out, and he chose me. He pitched me in and I did more than alright on Johnny Hughes.

We lost 1-13 to 1-10. By the end of the year, however, I had my All-Ireland medal when the Mayo under-21s drew with Derry in the middle of October, and then went up to Irvinestown and defeated them two weeks later, 1-8 to 1-5.

I never got a chance to celebrate the win as the army had decided that I needed an extra lesson in life.

It wasn't slobbering that led to me being disciplined.

It was a green biro.

IN THE ARMY during my cadetship, if you wished to do anything or go anywhere, you needed to make a written application.

A 'scrianta', it was called commonly by us.

If you wanted to pop down to the shop to buy a pair of laces, you needed your scrianta. Without that piece of paper, you were going nowhere.

It was the final weekend in October, a Bank Holiday, and we were all being let out on the Saturday morning. We didn't have to hightail it back to the barracks until Monday evening. A whole weekend, and on the Sunday I was playing in the All-Ireland under-21 football final replay.

I'd spent the week learning how to ride a horse. A week in Equestrian School was one of the easier weeks in a cadetship, and I was fluting around on the Friday afternoon when one of the other cadets told me that 'they' were looking for me.

'YOUR SCRIANTA... IT'S NOT IN!' he shouted over to me.

I knew how to write one in double quick time.

I ran into another lad's room, and found a pen. I ruled out the sheet of paper, perfectly, and just as 'they' liked and I slept happily that night, awaiting a full three days out of sight of the army. The next morning, on parade, with everyone bursting to go and everyone spotless, my name was called out.

The training officer was not happy with me.

Though all I heard were the words... 'GREEN PEN!'

What?

What's he just said?

'NOW... CADET McSTAY!'

I tried to stand as tall as I have ever stood in my life.

I stared straight ahead.

'NOW...' he continued.

'CADET McSTAY... YOU WILL NOT BE GOING TO ANY ALL-IRELAND FINAL... UNTIL SUNDAY MORNING.

'YOU... CADET McSTAY... YOU WILL ALSO BE BACK HERE AT 10 O'CLOCK ON SUNDAY NIGHT!'

Dermot Earley, as decent a man as ever walked into the army, did all he could for me but there is no shifting a decision in the military once it has been made. And when we won the game and I wanted to join my teammates for our celebration, Dermot tried again.

The bonfires had to be lit without me.

Dermot had picked me up in The Curragh and drove me to the game, and he also brought me back to the barracks by 10 o'clock on the Sunday night.

Bank Holiday Monday morning I met a NCO with a bucket and scrub at his feet.

There were four of us. And four buckets, four scrubs.

He pointed at the metal staircase.

'I want it shining!' he ordered.

◊ ◊ ◊ ◊ ◊

DONEGAL DIDN'T WORRY us all that much.

Long before we got back home to Roscommon, and got off the team bus after losing to Tyrone, we'd worked out that we had every chance of winning game two in the Super 8s.

Donegal were without Paddy McBrearty.

Even when they had McBrearty, the first time we played them in the league in 2016, up there, in Letterkenny, and McBrearty kicked six points from frees, we'd beaten them by five. 1-19 to 0-17.

They beat us by a point in the Hyde in the league in 2017.

But we could have won that one, too. Near the very end Ronan Stack had a great chance. The game was in injury time. A point would have put us one up. Ronan went for his goal. His shot was saved, and they went straight down the field to score the winner. 2-9 to 0-16.

After the game, Liam asked Ronan why?

'Why not take your point?'

I liked his answer. I loved his answer in truth, because it told me he was not only a brilliant young footballer, but that he was also a brave footballer. A thinking footballer.

'I wanted to put it in the net,' he explained. 'I knew they'd have another chance... I didn't want them to go down and get a point to level it!'

Ronan Stack wanted to win the game, for sure, when he had his chance. And all our lads believed they had a right to win against Donegal.

Donegal were no Tyrone. They were no Dublin or Mayo, they were a team with a new manager and in transition.

We were at home.

Even after a heavy defeat, Roscommon could always bounce back. Big, bad defeats did not leave Roscommon on the floor. We were well used to getting a right battering and still coming out of our corner the following week.

It's how it's always been for Roscommon teams.

The Tyrone defeat in round one of the Super 8s was bad. It was horrible and humiliating, but within 24 hours it was out of our system.

Easy.

Roscommon footballers know there will be days when they may be torn apart. It's part and parcel of life for a Roscommon footballer. None of the lads ever threw the towel in at the end of a day like that. Heavy defeats and big, comeback performances. That's actually the life of a Roscommon footballer.

We won the Connacht title in 2017 after losing six out of our seven games in the league and getting relegated. Being murdered one Sunday? Being absolutely destroyed?

It was never something we weighed up in our hearts.

Or kept in our heads for long.

DONEGAL?

They've lost to Dublin... if we beat them and... Dublin beat Tyrone?

We're level with Tyrone.

Two points each... and we've got Dublin in our final game?

It's Super 8s, but it's a rubber match for Jim Gavin.

He'll put out a weakened team in the final round of games... and if we win... we're on four points.

We can get through this.

The All-Ireland semis... they're not out of the question.

If Dublin put out the poorest team they've got?

Gavin drops his guard?

'LADS...

'LISTEN... WE STILL HAVE THIS IN OUR HANDS!'

Dreaming again!

THE MIND OF a manager is a place for simple maths and the strangest concoctions. It's not a rational place.

It's a place where there are always possibilities.

Has to be like that! Otherwise, how can a manager look into all the faces circling him in the dressing-room, and how can he utter words that he simply has to let loose?

It's a place where there always has to be some hope.

I made myself believe that Roscommon would defeat Donegal in game two of the Super 8s. And I believed that we would get one shot at defeating Dublin in game three, and that we'd take that shot, even if it was a long shot. We'd get damned close to them.

Surprise the whole country.

2016

1

MONAGHAN 2-10 ROSCOMMON 1-9
NFL DIVISION ONE (ROUND 1)
KILTOOM
JANUARY 31

THE YEAR WOULD close with my friendship with Fergal O'Donnell also ended, and broken into two pieces. Of all the results I chased in 2016, that was the last one I wished for, but it was unavoidable.

Fergal is one of the true leaders in Roscommon football.

He was a giant on the field and, in the eyes of most people who love and respect Roscommon, he never shed that appearance even when he retired. When the championship would come to an end in late July, when we would be run off our feet by Clare in a round four qualifier, whipped by six points in Pearse Stadium, the pair of us would meet up less than a handful of times in the town. In my home, in coffee shops, in the county board offices. There would be no row, no angry words at all.

The final time, we would shake hands, and we would get to talk on another couple of occasions over the phone and then, nothing.

Not a word has passed between us since.

In one full football season, which did not even extend itself to 12 months, our friendship which had been 20 plus years in the making, beginning when I agreed to play with Roscommon Gaels, captain them to a county title, later manage them to a county title first time of asking while Fergal manfully forced it to happen out on the field… at the end of one fast season, we would be left walking through the same town and acting like total strangers.

I was the one who asked him to join me on my management team. I asked him to come on board as a selector, before agreeing to roles of joint managers after some discussions. The two of us, and three selectors.

And I alone was the one who decided it was over. I had to take a hammer to the same management team. It was the toughest act I would have to carry out in all my years in football.

THE 2016 SEASON began so eagerly.

We decided to throw everything we had at it, at the best teams in Division One. And we beat Kerry in Killarney, went down to Pairc Ui Rinn and had 18 points to spare over Cork. We went up to O'Donnell Park in Letterkenny and were five points a better team than Donegal. More than that, in truth. We survived in Division One. Easily, and for the most part we enjoyed ourselves.

We reached the league semi-finals, but by the end of the first-half of the season I knew it was not working out. I was not getting onto the field the team I wanted to get onto the field.

Neither was the team playing the way I wanted Roscommon to play. And yet, Fergal and I worked hard together through the winter and spring.

From the beginning, we were the last two men standing at the end of most of those cold winter nights, whether we were training in Kilbride or Tarmonbarry, or back in St Brigid's which was the one ground that was a home from home for me. The county had no training home of its own.

There are no floodlights in Hyde Park, and only in the lengthening evenings of the early summer did it open its doors to the team.

There were so many nights in Kilbride when Fergal and I found ourselves at midnight, closing up the place. We agreed that we should always see to it that the boys were back on the road for home by a quarter past 10. The management team would then sit down and talk. Then, finally, it was Fergal and me.

In the black of the country. The field in absolute darkness, the floodlights turned off an hour and a half earlier. The two of us, talking as we locked up the outhouses and the dressing-rooms.

The wind and the perishing rain all that winter were unrelenting. And after locking up, I'd have to place the key in its secret location in the distance and amble back to my car, barely able to see where I was going.

Fergal had longer to travel home then me. He had to head to Boyle. I only had to run back into Roscommon, but Fergal would be waiting in his car as I went to swing the big heavy gates closed, and got to work on the chains locking it tighter still, my fingers freezing over and fumbling with their final duty of the long evening. After I had locked and chained the gates, and before I made my way to the hiding place for the keys, Fergal liked to lower his car window and ask me the same question.

'I wonder how Jim Gavin gets on with the gates... up in Dublin?' he'd ask me, struggling to hold back his big deep laugh before arriving at the word... 'Dublin'.

IT WAS ALL about Monaghan in our heads, in those first few weeks as we waited for the season to start. We ended up meeting them in Kiltoom, in round one of the National league.

Hyde Park was closed to us because of the state of the pitch, and it would remain closed to us. We would end up playing 13 competitive matches in 2016, and only get two of them at home. It was nuts. By the time we got to play Sligo in the Connacht championship we'd played the previous 10 games at different venues. We wanted a winning start to our year.

Me? I wanted to be as successful as a county manager as Malachy O'Rourke in Monaghan. To do that, we had to announce ourselves as a new group. A new Roscommon. We were not going to get thrown around.

That's what Monaghan had done. Stood up for themselves.

For several years, despite being a small county like Roscommon, and having a similar population, same number of clubs, I guess, Monaghan had made it clear that they were not going to be fucked around by anybody.

As a commentator and analyst, I had always admired O'Rourke's regime and his personal attitude. He takes no messing from his own men, or rival teams. He wants his men to be ferociously physical. What he has achieved with his group of footballers is something magnificent.

Why wouldn't Roscommon wish to be Monaghan?

Like them, why wouldn't we too decide to get our hands dirty, and make ourselves competitive and make ourselves at home as a Division One football team?

In Kiltoom, the conditions on the afternoon were truly shocking.

I wasn't down on the sideline.

Instead, I was up in the press box. We'd agreed that Fergal should take the line and the 'bainisteoir' bib in all our games.

The game should not have been played. The conditions were dire, and quite dangerous, but nobody in our dressing-room was waiting around for the referee to call off the game. It seemed we had been waiting forever, for Monaghan.

It was a game of turnovers.

Thirty-one of them from us alone.

The following week, we would go even better on our personal best for turnovers when we registered a total of 41 against Kerry. All through the season, all of our good work needed to be doubly good because we kept turning over the ball to the opposition.

It was also a game we should have won. We lost by four points, 2-10 to 1-9, but we had it just about wrapped up at one stage.

Still, it was 1-8 each after 63 minutes.

At half-time, we had been six points up, 1-5 to 0-2, but when they came back out for the second-half they decided to push right up on our kick-out. O'Rourke knew he had let us get too much of our own ball. Dessie Mone and Fintan Kelly took charge of operations for them, and Colin Walsh wasn't bothered playing as a tight corner-back anymore.

Stephen Bohan, one of our three selectors, had done excellent work for weeks in refining our kick-outs, and in the first-half Darren O'Malley was getting everything away perfectly. The lads in front of our goalkeeper were stacked up the middle of the field, like a crucifix. In that huddle we were ready to make our runs. We weren't innocent either, we were also ready to do some holding on the Monaghan forwards.

But O'Rourke saw enough of that business and dealt with it during half-time. Their aggression levels were definitely raised in the second-half, but the game left me with two memories in particular.

The first was the goal they scored in the final minutes to rip the game from our arms. Darren had tried to kick another short one. He dinked it out to Neil Collins, our full-back and he went down over it. But Neil didn't see the ball hit a divot. The ball never came up off the ground for him, but went straight to their danger man. And, in a flash, Conor McManus had the ball in the back of our net.

MY SECOND MEMORY from our defeat in Kiltoom was longer lasting and came from a free, in their half.

One of their forwards, Dermot Malone, not a big man at all but a busy little fella, always tackling, forever making a nuisance of himself, actually made sure they sewed up the game.

He did so by making one big, physical play.

He was marking Ronan Stack. And just as the ball was about to be kicked, Malone grabbed Ronan and threw him to the ground.

Malone then collected the ball.

Half a minute later they kicked their insurance point.

The incident also enforced my belief that linesmen choose to do nothing much, or at least do nothing much to make themselves seen or heard, in the final 10 minutes of a game.

During the first 15 minutes, they are onto everything. But when the game comes down the finishing straight they leave all the big decisions to the referee.

We knew it would be a rough, tough game. We were prepared for late belts, and the odd dirty one perhaps. Thankfully, Roscommon are no angels when it comes to fighting a corner either.

One thing I always loved about Roscommon teams down through the years was their backbone, and their refusal to walk away from games that develop a nasty streak. Roscommon, as a football team, are prepared to go to war when necessary, and even on occasions when it is not necessary.

On the Tuesday evening after the defeat, we stopped at the Malone incident and stayed there for some time during our video analysis. We told Ronan he could never again let an opponent get away with one of the easiest acts in the book.

The warning was extended right across the room.

2

ROSCOMMON 0-13 MAYO 0-10
FBD PROVINCIAL LEAGUE
CASTLEBAR
JANUARY 17

TWELVE MONTHS BEFORE being appointed manager of Roscommon, I was the only man nominated to take over the job in my county of birth. James Horan had resigned fast enough after Mayo had lost an amazingly courageous All-Ireland semi-final replay against Kerry in Limerick and, for the second time in my life, the Mayo job was mine.

Or so it seemed.

On each occasion, it was me or nobody.

Each time, the county board chose nobody, and I've never kidded around by pretending that I was not hurt personally on each occasion. When I sat in front of the main men on the Mayo county board in September of 2014 I knew they were not going to give me the job. Even though my stock as a manager could not have been higher.

I had managed Roscommon minor and Mayo under-21 teams, and brought the under-21s to an All-Ireland final. I had managed and won county titles in Roscommon with three different clubs, and I had led St Brigid's to the All-Ireland title on St Patrick's Day in 2013.

I wanted to be Mayo manager.

I wanted the job with practically every single fibre in my body. Second time around, I had a first and final meeting with key members of the board in Kiltimagh before, as I understood it, my appointment would be signed off and announced. But I knew early on in that meeting. There was no sense of any warmth in the room, never mind some curiosity and excitement. We all want to feel 'wanted' when we start a new role in life.

I had no sense that I was the man that Mayo wanted.

There were no eyes lighting up in heads. Instead, it was heads down, as notes were taken in an everyday, business-like sort of manner. I had all the ideas, all the data in front of me. I had my plan to finish off James Horan's brilliant body of work and make Mayo All-Ireland champions and let everyone in the county have a good, hearty winter's sleep, at last.

The whole episode left me slightly traumatised, which may appear dramatic, but I had a deep wish to prove myself on the sideline as a county manager, standing beside the big boys, the smartest of the smart. I always felt that county would have to be Mayo.

I didn't say very much publicly at the time. There was a lot of publicity, and it was negative noise which always makes me edgy and, nearly always, I walk away from difficult situations like that and keep my counsel to myself.

The Mayo board basically let it be known that I had big plans alright, but they were also expensive plans which would simply break the bank.

I'd been contacted by others. Longford, Sligo and Kildare had had a word with me over the years, but our conversations ended early. I was being courteous. Then, in the late summer of 2015, I got a phone call out of the blue.

It was a private call from a Roscommon GAA official. He wanted to know my thoughts on taking over as Roscommon manager. I replied that Roscommon already had a manager, and one who was doing a pretty good job.

John Evans was still Roscommon team boss.

'But... what if?'

That was the question left with me.

IT WAS NOT something I felt at all comfortable with, even contemplating the notion privately.

If I answered with a 'yes' to the question, I might be seen to be acting in a sinister manner, and if I said 'no'? I didn't say 'no'.

In more ways than one, I had been asked, 'What if...?'

I knew nothing much about John Evans, only that he was from Kerry and was putting in the hard yards as Roscommon manager. He had taken the team from Division Four to Three, from Division Three to Two, and from Division Two to One in double quick time and I felt he deserved his day in the sun in Division One.

There were more phone calls.

The caller was worried that the county would end John Evans' days as manager, and that they would then be left with nobody on hand to immediately take over from him. 'What if there was a vacancy?' I was asked, 'Would you take it... would you take the job?'

The following week, the executive of the Roscommon county board met and proposed John Evans as manager, and put his name forward to the board delegates for a formal sign-off. Between the proposal and ratification of the appointment, Evans resigned. He later explained that he understood there was a move against him, and that he had been informed that he did not have the support of the incoming county board chairman.

It was not a way for a county to do its business.

It was messy.

Plus, it was hardly fair on a man who had done his best for the county. Then again, in my 30 years living in Roscommon I have witnessed at first hand a county which has specialised in beheading managers. There were good men before John Evans who also were informed, without any great fanfare or notice of any kind, that their time in the job was up.

THERE WAS A vacancy.

And so, I met with the county board.

St Brigid's put my name forward. I wanted it, but I also wanted to feel secure in the job and after seeing how John Evans was dealt with in the end, I did not wish to make my appointment high risk. Other managers like Evans did not live in the county. Him and those before him were able to go home when their tenure ended. I was different, I was living in Roscommon.

Roscommon was going to remain my home.

I saw Fergal O'Donnell as a man I could work with. He was well known to me, and as a former star midfielder and a former manager who had captained and managed the county to Connacht titles in the recent past, I also saw Fergal as someone who would help make the new management team bomb-proof.

I was sure we would work well together.

'NOW LADS... THIS is not a coronation!'

Those were the opening words from the out-going chairman of the county board. Michael Fahey was seated directly in front of Fergal and myself, and either side of the chairman were Karol Mannion and Stephen Lohan.

Lohan had been one of Fergal's former players. Mannion was with me in St Brigid's. And the two of them were now interviewing the pair of us.

It was not wrong, but it felt strange and that was before we were warned that there was going to be no 'coronation'.

WE TORE INTO the job.

We wanted to have more work done than any other team in Division One, and we managed that. Our first big day out was in Castlebar. It was only an FBD league match, but Roscommon had not beaten Mayo in the championship since 1986, and I have no idea when they had last beaten Mayo in any kind of game in MacHale Park.

It was a big game for me.

It was Mayo.

And they had a new manager, too. Stephen Rochford was a former corner-back for me in my first year as Mayo under-21 manager. I am a huge admirer of him as a manager, and he'd the guts to take over the Mayo job after the players had made it known that they wanted an end to the management of Noel Connelly and Pat Holmes after just 12 months.

Amongst other things, co-managers in Mayo was deemed unsatisfactory.

There was a big crowd watching us all at work in MacHale Park. I was up in the stand. Fergal was on the sideline, but I felt just as many eyes on me, and it felt bloody good to win. Our communication all through the match was also smooth and perfectly satisfactory.

I'd gone to Longford to buy the radio system I wanted. Using my knowledge from my years in the Signal Corps in the army, I'd no excuse not to have us all on the correct page at all times, whether it was the medical channel or the management channel.

We built a strong management and backroom team, which quickly totalled 23 in number. Fergal had been superb in getting the best people, starting with talking Martin Daly back in as our team doctor. Our physio and recovery team was led by Ashling Creighton. We had excellent Athletic Training Therapists. Our masseuses were the best. We had a stats team who were exceptional. Sean Finnegan, my best friend, was overviewing this and all of the team's logistics.

Before a serious game of football had been played in 2016, it looked like we were flying. But it would also be a help to start winning games, and coming out of Castlebar and heading home it was good not to have lost. We also drove out of Castlebar in our magnificent new yellow bus, all shiny and state-of-the-art, all quarter of a million euros worth or thereabouts, I'm told.

In a county with hardly a seat in its pants, it was strange to be perched high in such a Fancy Dan vehicle. For starters, there was no chance of doing something nice and quietly, and secretly, anywhere in the country once we were spotted leaving Roscommon in a bus that looked as powerful as an elephant-sized Ferrari.

Lose a few matches, and I could just imagine the voices.

'Jaysus lads.

'Did you see the poor auld innocents…

'In their big, swanky, shiny bus… God Almighty, they'll make a holy show of us before this is all over!'

LIAM McHALE AND I had our first official disagreement after we lost to Galway in the FBD final. He was right. I was wrong. We went to Tuam, and we made a hames of the game. There was only one point in it, in the end, 2-8 to 0-13 in their favour, and afterwards Liam reminded me of something John Maughan came out with ad nauseum.

'Beat Galway and Roscommon, as often as we can… every time we see them!'

That was Maughan's firm belief as Mayo manager and Liam could not understand why we had selected a car load of players for the game whom we had already decided we'd most likely release from the squad a few days later. We had to trim the squad for the league.

'What the hell are we doing?' Liam demanded of me.

'We're playing lads in a final, and… three days later they're not even going to be on the panel?

'What message is that sending out?'

Yeah, he was totally right. Galway took a grip on the game early on after Damien Comer scored two goals in typical Comer style.

I had one eye on Monaghan seven days later in our opening league game. I should have seen Galway for what they were, because Galway were the first team standing in our path and determined to stop us from getting to be the team we wanted to be. After them, we'd Mayo to deal with, but Galway were first.

And, it would turn out that Galway were the team who never disappeared from that pathway. It was Galway we would fight longest and hardest against in my three years. Three Connacht finals were left down to the pair of us to share out. Kevin Walsh, more than anyone else, would be the manager I needed to out-think, out-manoeuvre… simply get out of my way.

AND, OF COURSE, three days after the defeat by Galway there I was sitting down in my office in my home with the names and numbers of a gang of lads I had to call. Lads who had trucked through the mud with us for the previous few months, lads we had given one last look over by selecting them on the team for the FBD final.

It was not our cleverest week.

I hated calling them.

I got better at it in season two and three, but making those calls always left my stomach in a knot. Two, three hours and by the end of it, always, I was physically and mentally wrecked.

3

ROSCOMMON 0-14 KERRY 1-10
NFL DIVISION ONE (ROUND 2)
KILLARNEY
FEBRUARY 7

BEFORE I EVEN left the dressing-rooms in Kiltoom after our first league game, I was already thinking of Kerry one week later. In fact, I was weighing up how it would feel to be driving back up north from Kerry after losing our first two league games.

Kerry were an All-Ireland winning team.

Eamonn Fitzmaurice was an All-Ireland winning manager, and Roscommon had not won down there in a few hundred years, I guessed. It was actually worse than that, I discovered in the days before the game. Roscommon had never won a game of football in Kerry. Not once.

Fitzmaurice had brought his lads up to Croke Park a week earlier and been beaten by Dublin, by two clear goals. They'd be hungry.

And they were. It was windy and tricky in Fitzgerald Stadium, but they had three points on the board in the opening nine minutes.

We had the breeze at our backs.

But, after that point from Johnny Buckley and two frees from Barry John Keane, we tightened up at the back and didn't give them another score for 19 minutes.

We scored the next eight points.

We made it look like we had gone down there for some shooting practice, starting with Enda Smith kicking our first point in the 10th minute.

Immediately, we settled.

Cathal Cregg levelled up the game in the 17th minute, after Donnachadh Walsh had hit the post at the other end and we swept the ball down the field. Cregg and Ciarán Murtagh were running circles around their opponents, and when Cian Connolly put the ball over on the rebound in the 25th minute we were sitting pretty.

0-8 to 0-3.

I was sitting high in the stand.

I could see Fergal and Liam at work, and I also found it hard enough to take my eyes off Fitzmaurice 20 yards away from them.

He was the picture of calm, as usual.

Keane scored his third free in the 27th minute.

Tommy Walsh added another.

Three minutes before half-time, Darren O'Sullivan found Stephen O'Brien who finished off a 35 metres run from underneath the stand by finding the back of our net.

Buckley scored the last point of the half.

0-8 to 1-6.

AS A CO-COMMENTATOR with RTE for 20 years, I understood the benefits of watching a game from on high, and far removed from the hustle and bustle of the sideline.

With St Brigid's, I usually took to the stands.

I had no doubts about that decision.

I also felt that most referees might not like the look of me on the sideline in a bainisteoir bib. Even if one or two of them glanced over at me, and only saw RTE's *Sunday Game* man either shouting out orders or standing there and looking far too content with himself, it might not be of any help.

Lots of people disagreed with my decision.

Friends, confidantes, lots of folk listening to the bullshit and trying to decipher it for me, came to the conclusion quite quickly that I should be seen to be leading the team. Not hiding away high up in the stand.

Hiding?

More than one person warned me that I could be accused of hiding, and then mooching away after a defeat without anyone getting to look at me.

Loyal supporters would want to see me and have their say.

Clowns too.

They all paid their good money to look me up and down during a game.

And especially afterwards.

That's what I was told.

But I had made up my mind that I would not deny myself the benefits of watching the whole game, same as I had done with RTE year after year, and seeing everything in the calm of the clouds. I stuck to my guns.

FERGAL TOOK THE half-time talk in Fitzgerald Stadium.

That's how we agreed to do it. I'd talk before the game, Fergal would talk at half-time. Also, Liam and myself would spend five minutes with the forwards during the half-time period. David Casey and Stephen Bohan would take the backs. And Fergal would talk with the midfielders, before also talking to the whole room.

We had our stats from the first-half.

We were calm enough.

We'd taken a good few blows from Kerry in the final minutes of the half, but a sense of adventure remained. And that was important. We'd come down to Kerry on an adventure. It had been 13 years since Roscommon had played Kerry anywhere in the league, and we were excited as we took in a tidy training spin after our journey down the day before.

We all knew Killarney.

I'd seen a lot of the magnificence of Fitzgerald Stadium, thanks to my RTE duties, and the splendour of the mountains, and their glory and gracefulness in the distance, is something that always took me by surprise. Most of the Roscommon lads had only viewed the stadium on their TV screens and mainly on perfect blue-skied summer days.

We were all in thrall in many different ways.

Mostly, we all felt honoured to be running out onto the field.

Meeting Kerry.

In their great home.

For me, crossing the field after the game, I came across Eamonn Fitzmaurice doing an interview with TG4. That was also a pinch myself moment.

But I pinched a version of myself that was 10 feet tall. I was managing a county team. I was co-manager of the Roscommon team that had come down to Kerry and defeated them for the first time.

I'd watched our lads plant the Roscommon flag in Kerry soil.

THE FIVE OF us had worked the room hard at half-time.

Kerry were that one point in front.

And they had the breeze to come in their favour.

'They will not have the heart for a fight!'

That's what we told our lads. It's not something that many opposing managers could ever lay at the feet of a Kerry team, but there was a chance that Kerry might think they had seen the best of us in that first-half. And that they had still done enough to show us we were second best before the half-time whistle sounded.

It was worth a shot, convincing our lads that Kerry would not have the heart for a surprise battle.

'We've got to test them…we've got to see!'

WE WON THE second-half of the game, 0-6 to 0-4.

I jumped three steps at a time to get down onto the field when the final whistle sounded. At the very end they had one brilliant last chance, but they made a ridiculous fumble. The Longford referee, Fergal Kelly also gave us one or two nice calls in the second-half, which is unusual when an underdog meets Kerry.

It's Kerry, especially at home, who nearly always get the decisive nod.

Kerry played an open style in that half, and we tucked in more defensively, developing the roles of our two wing men and asking them to drop back into deeper positions. We dug in, but we also played the ball with a fluid style.

I was so proud.

But I could not help myself thinking about the 41 turnovers. To cough up possession that number of times? It meant we had to work twice as hard as necessary to win the game. And, if we had totalled half of that number?

We might have taken Kerry by a handful of points in their own home.

These were strange, but amazing thoughts to have swirling around in my head as I put the same head back against my high seat on our bus, a bus that finally had a team deserving of a smooth and luxurious delivery back home.

I looked at the lads throwing all of our nutritional advice out the window. We stopped in Nenagh to eat, but they were still hungry. With my head back, I watched them come back onto the bus after one stop at a petrol station with hands full of choc ices and Mars bars. With my head back, I listened to the sports announcers on the radio… 'Wait till you hear this result from Killarney this afternoon!'

I WAS PROUD of every one of them.

Especially our full-back, Neil Collins. He had made a costly mis-judgment a week earlier against Monaghan, but now he had held Tommy Walsh to a single point. And he had watched Walsh leave the field by the end.

Neil is an eclectic sort of young man.

He loved his gym work, but he was also into photography and career-wise he was ready to start in the fashion industry. He would tear his hamstring right off the bone a few months later in training. A Connacht semi-final against Sligo would be his last ever game for Roscommon.

The injury helped him to make up his mind to move to New York and pursue his career there, and also line out for his adopted city against Leitrim in the championship. Neil was also a very good listener.

Liam spent more time with Neil than anyone else the evening before the game. He wanted Neil to play Tommy Walsh as though the pair of them were out on a basketball court together. We were most worried about Walsh destabilising our whole defence by winning and breaking high ball.

Liam wanted Neil to think of Walsh as an armchair.

'Lie into him…lie into him low!' Liam ordered.

'Lie back in there, and make sure he has no room to jump over you… got me? Nice and low into him… with your arse!

'Then pull the chair…'

'Walk out on him.

'You'll stop him getting the ball every time!'

BY HALF PAST 10, I was sitting on a stool myself.

I was in my local, Down The Hatch on Church Street in Roscommon town and I had the first of two pints of Coors Light on order. It's a place where you can meet nobody and everybody on a Sunday night.

I had decided when I took the job that I would not deprive myself of my couple of hours there on a Sunday night, not unless I was absolutely shattered tired. Otherwise, win or lose, I decided I'd be there.

In the company of Seamus Hayden and Larry Brennan, both of them my friends and the owners. Tony McManus might also swing in on Sundays. It's a place where mostly decent, calm Roscommon supporters can talk without anyone getting too excited.

It's a GAA HQ in many ways.

I had no intention of walling it off from my new life as Roscommon team manager. Win or lose! There would be no picking and choosing when to appear in The Hatch.

I wanted to remain comfortable with the huge job I had taken on board, or as comfortable as humanly possible. Maybe my view was simplistic, and there was an innocence perhaps in some of the things I said to the players, but I dearly wanted all of us to do our level best, and enjoy our time together knowing that we were giving it our very best shot on behalf of the people of Roscommon.

'Give it one hundred per cent… that's all we have to do!'

That was my most valuable piece of advice.

And it was advice I was determined to take on board, too.

'You might find that we are not good enough,' I continued, '… that you're not good enough… that I'm not good enough.'

Undoubtedly, we were all about to find out.

In one year, or two or three years or beyond?

'But, if we don't give one hundred per cent… we'll never know!'

4

ROSCOMMON 1-19 DONEGAL 0-17
NFL DIVISION ONE (ROUND 5)
LETTERKENNY
MARCH 13

IT WAS LIKE going to the moon to play a game of football.

Letterkenny is not all that far away. However, for young Roscommon footballers who had never been in the town in their lives, who had absolutely no reason to take a bus up there and spend a whole day amongst the locals, Letterkenny was something like Killarney.

A mystery, and another big adventure.

We'd arrived in Letterkenny on the Saturday and had a run-out that evening.

The next afternoon the lads were running onto a field they barely knew had existed before the spring of 2016.

O'Donnell Park.

There was a huge crowd waiting for us. Also, we had Donegal, who even if Jim McGuinness had vamoosed to Glasgow to pursue a new career with Celtic, remained the game's deepest thinkers. Donegal had re-thought Gaelic football.

My respect for McGuinness and mostly everyone who had been around him, and for those who still remained on the field and on the sideline, was absolute. Of course, I was a little fearful. We had beaten Kerry, and then gone back south and annihilated Cork. We had made it three smart wins by seeing off Down. We were going to lose to somebody.

For a full month, Donegal also had had a good long look at us.

WHILE I WAS both respectful and fearful, I still expected us to beat Donegal.

Even when I saw their team sheet.

Even when I saw them out on the field before the game. They were all there. Michael Murphy and another dozen household names. All of them outstanding footballers who had already done it all.

Donegal looked the strongest team we had faced all season.

A couple of weeks before, in Cork, on a beautiful spring day, blue-skied, on an impeccable surface, Cork had looked second rate. And Down, too, were having an entirely miserable league campaign and struggling to win any of their games.

We were still fuelled by what we had achieved in Kerry, and since that win in Killarney we had further developed our game analysis and match-ups. Every week we were passing on even greater detail to our lads about what they were doing and what they needed to do. We were demanding more from them.

Every little thing on the field was being watched.

Analysed.

Discussed, and corrected.

Left hand passes that should have been right hand passes.

Punts that should have been hand passes.

Hand passes that should not have been delivered.

Hand passes that were six inches too high.

Too slow.

Delayed.

We should have beaten Cork by more than 4-25 to 3-10. Eighteen points did us no favours. We gave away the three goals, and that actually worried me a bit. *Why are we conceding sloppy goals?*

As the league rolled out, I had spent more and more time standing back, as managers get to do in lots of professional sports, and look over the fence at what was going on. When Fergal had the room, I'd listen, and watch.

Are they all paying attention?

Who's clued in?

Is that fella up for it?

He looks edgy to me!

It was definitely Fergal driving it through that league campaign. He and the older players, whom he'd had as minors, were a natural fit. I was comfortable with that. It was working well.

I was delighted.

The football we were playing looked unreal at times. We were flying, and we were fluid in what we were doing. I worried only a little. But I asked myself were we doing too much, too early and would we have a price to pay for it in the championship?

I had to dismiss those questions just as quickly.

What choice had we?

After the manner in which Fergal and I had accepted our jobs? The dressing-room had experienced three promotions in three successive springs, and if the spring of 2016 saw Roscommon relegated from Division One and the players rounded up, and told to retrace their steps?

Roscommon could not be sent into reverse.

We might not be forgiven for that.

And, because of our determination to win and succeed in Division One, and because we had a first round championship game in New York coming down the tracks at us at the start of May, we did not have the time, or the inclination, to taper things off.

We did not see the cliff edge.

Or the scary fall awaiting us.

I'VE NO IDEA whose idea it was to head up to our seats in the stand, with note books in one hand, and Cornettos in the other. But the journalists in the press box thought Liam and I looked quite at ease with the afternoon in front of us.

The Cornettos?

I've never seen Mickey Harte caught munching on an ice cream with a game about to start. Never mind. We bossed the first-half. Ciaráin Murtagh summoned up the confidence which was primed within the whole team by getting an early ball, and brushing off the attention of Ryan McHugh with a proper shoulder. He then fed Niall Daly for his first point.

Everything else fell right into place after that.

We went high on the Donegal kick-outs, as discussed, and gave them no breathing room at all in their own half. We also rotated our inside forwards, while retaining Senan Kilbride as an old fashioned target man. There was no rocket science to it.

Seanie McDermott and Niall McInerney dared to break from deep in our defence at every opportunity, and Neil Collins was also on the move, shadowing Michael Murphy all over the field.

Getting all the match-ups just right had taken up so much of our time as a management group all through the preceding week. As a chess match, we had been decisive in making our primary moves, and in response? Rory Gallagher, who had stepped into the tight shoes of McGuinness, didn't hit us with very much, or at least nothing that caught us unawares.

Murphy had one point by half-time.

We'd hit just two wides. A key stat for the team.

For one of those, Niall Daly had a goal chance abegging. We were five points in front at half-time. Early in the second-half we'd increased that to 0-13 to 0-6. We'd expected to be hit with a whole different Donegal after the break, but it didn't happen.

During the warm-up in a big field at the back of the main stand, they'd trotted by us just after we had started.

Jesus Christ… they're huge!

And they were. Actually they were rippling in jerseys which may have been sized that little bit too tight on purpose. It was still impressive.

I found myself glancing in their direction more often than I should have. I also told myself that that was what a Division One team should look like. That's what All-Ireland champions, reigning champs or past champs, look like.

Donegal looked like a team who were also ready to win a second All-Ireland title, and then they started their own warm-up routines.

My…ohhhhh my!

Slick… slick, slick, slick.

I didn't see one ball dropped by them.

But, out on the field, we looked the more focused team and as I examined the game from high up in the stand, and viewed the action and inaction on the sideline, I came to the conclusion that when Jim McGuinness left them, Donegal's chance of winning a second All-Ireland title also went up in smoke.

On occasions, we counter-attacked them with the panache of a McGuinness team and in the 58th minute Cathal Cregg came off the shoulder of Senan Kilbride in one sweeping move and scored the goal that finally left Donegal in a heap. It was spectacular, but we still had to get everything just right in the final quarter and we were slow in doing so. Too damn slow for my liking, and on the Tuesday evening I expressed my unhappiness to the whole of the management team.

I WANTED TO bring Cathal Compton into the game.

Cathal was a big, raw midfielder from Strokestown who still had a lot to learn but, on the bus home, his performance gave me greater satisfaction than any single other factor in our performance. He immediately got down the line in the middle third and contested, and won kick-outs. Three of them he won cleanly.

Cathal is also a brave young man. He goes for everything, and he was also nice and tidy in how he used each ball he won. He didn't allow himself to get pushed around as the game was getting edgy and Donegal knew it was drifting from their grasp, fast.

Neither did he leave himself open to be lamped by anyone.

I trusted him, and he had reciprocated.

But, I could not understand how I ended up in a fight to get him onto the field. Liam saw that Niall Daly was beginning to blow hard, and needed to come off. It must have taken all of 10 minutes to get Cathal in.

'Lads…this is taking too long!' I announced to everyone down on the sideline.

Nobody down there seemed to share the same degree of urgency, however.

'Lads… you need to be up here, to see that Niall is not tracking back… make the change…let's do it!'

On the Tuesday, at our management debrief, I had more to say about the whole episode. I was told that there had been a sequence of different delays, but I was not having any of that.

It was the only time all season that the line appeared to me to be slow in taking instruction from me.

IT WAS THE last Sunday in March before we got to run out in front of our people at Hyde Park. Though the pitch was no better than it had been at any time the whole spring. It was basically a swamp.

But it was our swamp.

And, better still, we were hosting Mayo. We had all the form, and Mayo had shown nothing in 2016. The whole context of the game was that we had a chance to send Mayo down into Division Two, and their amazing record in remaining a top tier team for the guts of a quarter of a century was about to end at our hands.

It was a tantalising prize for so early in the season.

We had beaten them in the FBD league in Castlebar, and repeating that in the Hyde was not going to make us a better team than them. In fact, it was not even going to put us on a par with them, but it would close the gap.

The game should never have gone ahead. There was water flying up everywhere. Ten minutes in, we realised the conditions were shocking, but there was so many people heading to the Hyde from early morning from Mayo, and our supporters had been talking about the game all week. There was serious excitement in the town itself. There was no way anyone dared to call off the game.

We thought we were absolutely ready for them.

They also knew that and they came with the firm intention of putting us back on our backsides. They wanted to put down a marker, and in the process they also wanted to make sure they were not going anywhere near Division Two.

They achieved both results, and followed up with a routine victory over Down to see to it that they stayed put in Division One. It was hugely disappointing for us.

We failed to make any kind of statement against the one team we wanted, more than any other, to make a statement against. We had had our say against Kerry and Donegal, and we would also prove ourselves Galway's equal more than once in the three years ahead. Mayo, however, were No.1 on my 'To Do' list.

Roscommon as a team needed to stand up to them, and win in a meaningful contest with the whole country watching. I, too, had a deeply personal wish to prove myself as a manager against Mayo.

When Stephen Rochford named his team on the Friday, I saw that he had beefed things up considerably with his selection. We thought we had a great chance, nevertheless.

From the start, we got thrown around the place.

Physically.

It was no contest.

And, by the time we'd finish up our league campaign I was actually feeling that I had been beaten up as a manager.

I was left feeling a little out of my depth, in truth.

That's the only word I can use to describe it. The league left me in a place where I fully understood what I was trying to do, and how immense the challenge was. And how great an effort it was going to take. It was a daunting feeling, and it all began with Mayo.

As Roscommon do, and have always done, we got back up on our feet and dusted ourselves down before meeting Dublin in our final game in the group. The game was switched from the Hyde to Carrick-on-Shannon in a hurry on the Sunday morning. We got stuck into them and should have drawn. They won by a point, 1-13 to 1-12.

But, in the league semi-final, Kerry just tore us asunder. They made us pay for beating them in Killarney and they also made us rethink, from head to toe, everything we thought we had achieved that afternoon in their place. I'd said to Liam and others that beating Kerry that afternoon would be worth six months' work to us as a group, and I had believed that as we journeyed home.

Six months? Less than six weeks down the road, Kerry were merciless in showing me that my calculation was simply silly.

SOME OF MY good friends thought I was especially harsh in my assessment of the team, and ourselves on the sideline, when the league ended.

Maybe that is true.

But I decided from the very start to make only honest assessments of what I was doing and I could not go easy on anybody when the league finally finished. We didn't lay a glove on Mayo, and Kerry had us finished off before half-time.

I never wanted to see Roscommon in a game that was over halfway through. I wanted us to be competitive in the second-half, just like the first-half. That was not asking too much, in my estimation.

But in the final weeks of the league the difference between us as new boys, in Division One for the first time in 13 years, and the others was something shocking. The others had been fighting it out in Division One forever.

Division One is different.

I was only fully awakened to that when we played Mayo. That's where it started. We were beginning to feel we belonged and, then, overnight, I was asking myself what are we doing here?

5

MAYO 1-11 ROSCOMMON 1-7
NFL DIVISION ONE (ROUND 6)
ROSCOMMON
MARCH 27

I HAD BEEN 16 years working with RTE before stepping out of the commentary booth, and swapping it for a county sideline.

By and large, my colleagues on *The Sunday Game* were decent and fair in their combined assessment of what I was trying to do with Roscommon. Pat Spillane and Joe Brolly, of course, seemed to take a little bit of enjoyment from giving me a couple of clips across the ear, but that was fine. Pat and Joe like to keep the script edgy.

Besides, I was being honest in my own judgement of what I was doing, and I did not want anyone in RTE going easy on me just because they felt that was the thing to do with a former workmate.

I loved working with RTE. However, I did not have a moment's hesitation in walking away. My first day's work with the station I was in the esteemed company of the late Jimmy Magee, and I had the opportunity of working with some seriously talented and professional people. Ger Canning and Marty Morrissey are at the very top of the broadcasting game, and it was always an honour to team up with them. Darragh Maloney... exceptional at his job. Michael Lyster, Des Cahill, Joanne Cantwell... brilliant at their work, too.

At that stage, I would love to have co-commentated on an All-Ireland final, but that was not to be as RTE had Martin Carney as their first choice in that chair. I respect Martin hugely, and fully understood RTE's decision-making, but I would have liked one All-Ireland and that was my only small regret as I walked away. However, I finally got my reward in 2019 when I was asked to work on the final between Dublin and Kerry.

I NEVER FELT any pressure calling games. Some of the lads did not care for live commentary, which can be something of a high-wire act compared to half-time analysis or evening analysis when you have extra time to consider what you have seen, and get your thoughts in order. And make sure that you are talking sense.

Live is different.

There are so many cameras at work, and lots of different angles being covered. The viewers at home are seeing almost everything, and I always saw it as my job to help them see that little bit more. They may not have seen a dummy run to open up some space, or some technical skill, or the small nuance on a rule that was taken advantage of, perhaps.

Doing games live you do have the safety of a 'lazy switch' of course which gives you a few critical seconds to double-check some things, like did the player bounce the ball twice before shooting his point or not? It's good to be able to take a small amount of time out, even if it is only a couple of seconds. And not make a complete ass of yourself.

Looking back now, however, I fully understand that all of us working for RTE as Gaelic football commentators and analysts had no real understanding of the pressure people are under on the sideline. It's slightly different with RTE's hurling men, because you have Anthony Daly there, and Cyril Farrell and Liam Sheedy who have both managed county teams to All-Ireland titles.

The football bunch know less.

They all believe, much like the man and woman watching at home, that the team boss on the sideline is totally on top of what he is at, to begin with. They think that mostly everything is planned and rehearsed, and there is very little seat-of-the-pants decision-making. When the opposite is the case.

If you are winning by 10 or 11 points in a game, sure thing, you can take lads off and move things around, and make it all look like a piece of pie. In reality, for the largest portions of games involving all managers, in football and hurling, there is grand chaos.

Plan A does not work.

Plan B is redundant too.

Someone gets injured.

You're losing by two points when you thought you'd be four or five up.

Mostly everything is going not the way you and your management team had imagined it and you are in survival mode far earlier in games than anyone watching might even think.

I've heard managers being asked, 'What were you thinking at that point?'

And the manager will come out with some old guff.

Truth is, there was no question of him thinking anything.

He was running on instinct.

Guessing.

Smart guessing, but gambling all the same.

THANKFULLY, I HAVE forgotten ninety per cent of what I have ever said as a commentator. I take comfort that I have never been malicious in anything I said, or taken a cheap shot because it was the easiest shot to take.

In my writing, I cannot say the same thing. I was very unfair in things I wrote about Maurice Sheridan, the former Mayo forward who was one of the best free-takers in the country, and also Meath's three-time All-Ireland winner, Martin O'Connell. In the *Mayo News* I asked how Maurice could be so composed over the ball when taking free-kicks and seem to be all over the place when in possession?

It was an easy, inaccurate generalisation which did not fairly reflect on Maurice as a footballer, and even though we have spoken many times since, I still owe him an official apology. In the same paper I accused Martin of standing on someone's head, when I know now he would be the last man to ever act in that manner.

Martin, too, is due an apology. He was one of the most honest footballers who has played in the modern game.

I SOUGHT TO be professional, and fair and accurate, when sitting in that commentary booth all of those years. And I would always have started my 'homework' in the middle of the week, by looking at matches I'd saved or going onto YouTube.

Like the late and great Micheal O'Hehir, who knew his jockey colours off by heart and could get the names of horses out faster than anyone else in the business, I was always ready. There is a great distance between the commentary booth and the field of play, and I needed to know every single man out there without having to pause and check programmes or look for any help from someone else.

Driving up to Dublin the morning of a game, or the day before if I had other work on, I liked to check through the two teams, from No.1 to No. 26, sounding out a player's name against each number. Because of the distance from the field, most of the time high up in the stand all I am going to see is a dashing number.

I always wanted a name to every number. With all of that boxed away in my head, I liked to pull up to Croke Park by 11.30 am, park my car in the hotel across the road or else in the Davin car park and make my way up to the press room. I'd report to the Outside Broadcast unit and say a quick hello to the director and producer on duty, and the editor, and settle in with a coffee, and a gossip with Ger, Marty or Darragh.

I always had my highlighters at work.

Everything needs to be colour coded for my mind to relax into my work. My brief as a co-commentator, in the main, is to think tactical and technical. A bit like Roy Keane, I believe if I have failed to prepare, then I am prepared to fail in my duty to RTE and, more importantly, the television viewers. I have never felt good at flying by the seat of my trousers.

The different commentators have different wingmen who feed them with the all-important stats that are unfolding. Monsignor Eoin Thynne and Timmy McCarthy were with Ger. Marty relied on David Punch. All of them were invaluable sources of information from minute to minute and, for me, it was always important to cross-check my own notes with them at half-time and again after the game.

There never was one day in Croke Park when I have not felt it a privilege to be at work in the magnificent ground. It is a huge honour to be asked to talk to the whole nation, and arriving home at 7.0 or 8.0 pm in the evening I always feel that I have been part and parcel of a significant game that will go down in GAA history. Unless, of course, I am also doing the night show.

I was one of the few former players who felt comfortable going live and also offering analysis on the *Sunday Game* a few hours afterwards. If I was asked to do the later programme, I'd have to get up to Dublin earlier in the morning to review the games played the day before. That had me not getting home till midnight, or most commonly the following morning after staying overnight.

There are some weekends in June and July when there can be a dozen games played, and a lot of footage to be reviewed and sliced up.

That, I suppose, is the flip side of a supposed glamour role with RTE.

ARRIVING AT A ground, as an RTE man or as a manager of a county team, is an equal privilege in my eyes. It's seriously exciting being in the centre of the action.

For a home game in Hyde Park, we'd have all of the lads finished eating their pre-ordered meal in the Abbey Hotel, supervised by our dietician, by 11.15 am, 11.30 am at the very latest. In truth the lads never stopped eating. They were always ravenous, while myself and some of the management team would hardly eat anything. Stopping and sitting to eat only took up valuable time for me.

I'd let the lads go off for a walk then, or get onto their phones, before having them back in the team room in the hotel for 12.15 pm.

We'd spend the next 15 minutes running through everything one final time, re-emphasising what we were looking for, doubling down on the key match-ups. We would be on the bus by 12.50 pm.

I loved that short ride from the hotel. Presenting ourselves to the public, and moving through the crowd. That's when the sense of privilege is magnified.

On a team bus entering a ground you feel the chosen few, same as you feel specially chosen by RTE to commentate on the biggest games of the day.

We warmed up on a back pitch.

We were back into the dressing-room, and had final words.

And out by 1.35 pm.

Another warm-up on the pitch.

Counting down the vital minutes, and feeling the adrenalin flow that bit faster and with greater intention. Just like it always was for me in the RTE commentary booth with cans on my ears and a mic sitting on the shelf in front of me.

THERE WAS NO other football manager in the country as well prepared as I was for county management. My 16 years with RTE had me in the unique position where I had focused on, and broken down and analysed in the finest parts, pretty much every team in the country.

I was lucky to have all of that information stored up in my head.

Equally, I knew other grounds very well, and thought of Croke Park as a familiar work place, and all of that surely benefitted me. It was like I had been preparing for the moment of taking charge of Roscommon for most of my adult life.

And, still, the month of April, 2016, left me wondering, and asking myself if I was really able to do the job asked of me.

The serious job I was asking of myself.

AT ONE STAGE, after a flurry of scores immediately after half-time, Mayo were nine points in front of us. They led by only two points at the change, 0-6 to 0-4, but that told nothing of the story of the first-half.

They kicked 10 wides in the half, as they owned the ball and made as little of the treacherous conditions as they did of us. Ciaráin Murtagh had kicked two late points for us in added time before the break. Tom Parsons, and Aidan and Seamie O'Shea, owned the middle third of the field, and Parsons was also dropping back in front of his own full-back line and his tackling, his positional sense, was simply magnificent.

We had no answers out on the field.

Equally, as a management, it was like we were totally unprepared for what Mayo presented to us. We were looking at a Roscommon team that looked totally unprepared. We didn't get our first score until the 23rd minute from Conor Devaney, and the second-half was the same awful story as we did not get our first score of the half until the 58th minute from Fintan Cregg.

They should have had two goals in the first-half, but Geoffrey Claffey made two unbelievable saves from Diarmuid O'Connor and Lee Keegan. They had the wind at their backs in that half, but it made no difference when we changed ends.

They scored another point early, and then quickly enough Evan Regan summed up their technical and mental superiority in dealing with the ridiculous conditions by chipping the ball up to himself on the run, despite having Seanie McDermott on his back, and cutting onto his left foot and drilling the ball home. He had over-carried in the process, but we were unworthy of even making a big complaint to referee Maurice Deegan.

We brought the difference down in the closing 12 minutes and there were only three points in it at the end of normal time, but it was a game we were never going to win.

We deserved nothing from our day.

We had only embarrassed ourselves in front of our own people.

AFTER THE GAME against Dublin a week later, we received a standing ovation from the same Roscommon supporters. As a management team, I would have been happier if they had all remained seated.

We'd lost.

Bottom line, we had Dublin off balance, if you like. They were not at full strength with only nine first choicers starting. It was another dirty old day. The game was switched from the Hyde to Carrick-on-Shannon at 11.0 in the morning because of the deplorable state of our pitch and both teams, and all the supporters, were left a little at sixes and sevens having to make late arrangements.

I can't say I was happy after the game.

Ciaráin Murtagh missed with a free-kick in injury time to level the game. It was an opportunity he would normally have taken with his eyes shut, but he slipped as he struck the ball. He was unlucky, but he should have made sure not to slip.

He should have known to make sure, especially as he had been brilliant from start to finish all afternoon. He more than anybody saw to it that we

Joining the army and leaving the army after over three decades in uniform were two of the very best decisions I made in my life. Here I am on overseas duty in Lebanon in 2001 (above) and Kosovo in 2008.

My Dad (above) on his much loved bike in 1963 and my Mum eight years earlier on their honeymoon in Killarney.

My First Holy Communion Day.

My Mum with nine of us (two more still to arrive) in 1970 and with three of her boys and some of the treasure we'd won.

My Dad at another McStay wedding in 1984 (with Rory, me, Brian and Paul).

*Our engagement party in 1988
(me, Verona, Mum and Dad).*

*Emma giving
the camera
all of her
attention and
our pensive
twins, Megan
and Caoimhe
in 1999
(right).*

Verona's parents,
Howard and Vera (left)
who have played such
a vital role in our lives,
and Verona and myself
dressed up all fancy at
Adare Manor.

The 'Rossie McStays'
as we're called.

I feel I never achieved my potential in the Mayo shirt though I had one of my very best days against Dave Synnott of Dublin in the 1985 All-Ireland semi-final (bottom) when as you can see (right) I was a bit on the lean side.

The Mayo team that might have won the 1989 All-Ireland final had we not panicked against Cork in the final straight.

I got to work with a lot of teams as manager before taking up the role with Roscommon. I was the proudest man alive to manage Mayo to the All-Ireland under-21 final in 2001 (top), but my greatest success came thanks to St Brigid's who won the All-Ireland club title in 2013.

I walked the pitch before Roscommon met Dublin in the National league in Carrick-on-Shannon in 2016 (top) but in my first year with the team I tended to take to the stand during games.

With my Roscommon co-manager, Fergal O'Donnell before our last game in 2016 when we lost to Clare in round four of the All-Ireland Qualifiers.

Sharing that winning feeling with my management team of Ger Dowd and Liam McHale after we defeated Galway in the 2017 Connacht final.

Ciaráin Murtagh lifts the Nestor Cup after our huge victory over Galway in the 2017 Connacht final and (below) Enda Smith and Tadhg O'Rourke are lifted high up by adoring Roscommon supporters.

The lads march around the pitch before our defining Connacht final against Galway in 2018.

The 2018 Connacht final was my fourth crunch championship meeting with Kevin Walsh of Galway (right).

Remonstrating with the linesman during our tough loss to Donegal in the Super 8s in 2018.

For my trouble, after arguing with the linesman I had to spend the second half of that same game against Donegal removed from the pitch (above inset) and in the next game my suspension meant I was further removed to the Ballymore Box in Croke park when we were playing Dublin. My loyal lieutenant Sean Finnegan is on my right.

During my three years as Roscommon manager I got to fight it out with some of the best managers in the game, including Kevin Walsh, Stephen Rochford and also Dublin team boss, Jim Gavin (right).

Mickey Harte (top) and his team were one of the toughest nuts to crack, though I got the better of Kieran McGeeney and Armagh in my final year before bowing out against Declan Bonner and Donegal (left) in the last game in which I would have the honour of standing on the Roscommon sideline.

Despite the constant pressure and huge amount of work, what a joy and a privilege it was to be Roscommon manager. Here I stand (above) as close as I can to my former teammate and Rossie coach, Liam McHale as we are about to win the Connacht title in 2017. When it was all over I found myself back working for RTE and sitting back high up in Croke Park.

fought back from a 0-9 to 0-3 half-time deficit. The whole team fought like lions in that second-half. We had two men black carded. We got sucker-punched by a Dean Rock goal in the 63rd minute, two minutes after we had a good goal disallowed.

I could not have asked more from the dressing-room.

But, still, I was not happy. I wanted to get the Mayo loss out of our system, and only a victory over Dublin would manage to do that satisfactorily. Also, I was left wondering that same evening had Jim Gavin snubbed me before the game even started.

That thought irked me.

I had said hello to him as he passed me, and he did not even look down in my direction. I had been standing at a slightly lower height as he walked past with his management team. I mentioned it too Fergal and Liam at the time, and they told me to put it out of my head, and I did so.

I had coached Jim Gavin when he played for the Irish Defence Forces. We were on a three-weeks tour of Australia. Throughout the trip I found him a very quiet fella who kept a lot to himself, but we had talked lots at the same time.

After everything that had gone on all through the morning, it was hard not to shoot the breeze a little bit when we finally arrived in Carrick. I would always do so with officials from another county, or the groundsmen, if they said hello to me. Forty-five minutes before a run-of-the-mill league match for Dublin, I thought Jim Gavin would be equally relaxed.

But, no.

The Dublin management had business faces on.

No nonsense.

No selfies, or any other unnecessary shit from them, thank you.

They were already in their pre-game… 'process'. Their bubble.

But, I was pissed, even though I did not know for absolutely certain that Jim had even heard me say hello.

SENAN KILBRIDE HAD finished off a beautiful tapped goal to give us the momentum to really go after Dublin. We should have won it after that.

A draw with Dublin would have been something, and far bigger for us than a bloody good performance against Dublin. It would have been in the bank for another day. And after being tamed by Mayo, we needed to feel good about ourselves, and fast.

We had one major positive heading home. Niall McInerney had an unreal performance, and left us certain that we really had a top class player on our hands.

He had clearly eaten up all the stuff we had been feeding him, regarding training, and what he should be eating, and how seriously we wanted everyone to take their gym work. As a medical student with a lot of other information to pack into his head, it was invigorating and reaffirming for us as a management team to see how he did.

Niall loved the whole idea of playing for Roscommon, and clearly he saw only an upside to the hard work we were asking of him.

We had Kerry in the semi-finals of the league.

We were really looking forward to getting into Croke Park. 'This is where we want to be!' I told the team more than once in the week before the game. There was total truth in that.

I was counting up our opportunities to get to Croke Park. The league semi-final. The quarter-final of the championship. An away game against Dublin in the 2017 league. Three games, at the very least, and that is what we wanted.

We needed the experience of being there.

The exposure, and the pressure that comes with that. Besides, Croke Park is the mecca. It is where everyone wants to be, and that included me as manager. I wanted to manage in Croke Park, and be at the very top with all of the other team managers.

WE DIDN'T CHANGE anything for Kerry in the semi-final.

Our Nos. 10 and 12 knew they were in for a long day and that they had to give it everything they had in the tank, and make it to the 60th minute mark hopefully. Ciaráin Murtagh was going to have a big day's work at No. 11 also, dropping into the middle, and allowing one of our midfielders to drop back into the hole in defence. We were happy enough with that game plan. It had seen us get through the group stages okay.

Then Kerry buried us.

After losing to Mayo, I understood that we needed greater strength in the middle third, and we compensated by having Niall Daly and Fintan Cregg at work there, and they are two serious footballers, but they are still not huge men. They do not have that bulk under a dropping ball, which the likes of Aidan O'Shea takes advantage of. The Mayo size was something that I could not get out of my head.

It remained living with me for weeks.

When the league was over, I was also left with another memory that troubled me. A lot of lads had arrived onto the team coach heading to Croke Park for the league semi-final with their 'dancing clothes' in one bag and their playing gear in the other bag. I was annoyed by that. Some of the lads had decided that they would be staying overnight in Dublin after the game. I had anticipated that we'd all be back on the bus heading west.

The bus was far less than half full when we took off for home.

There's nothing worse than a miserable bus, with hardly anybody on it. I made up my mind that I would have a lot to say about it on the Tuesday evening. It was a bad defeat and we had a trip to New York right around the corner, and we needed to sort ourselves out. Fast. I was feeling the pressure. I didn't spare the lads.

I knew in my heart that they had put an awful lot into the FBD league and the National League, and the two months of heavy work that came before that. They had given us everything as a management group for six months, and they clearly thought that they deserved a blow out in Dublin before the championship started. And I could understand that. It was the optics that disturbed me.

We had been massively motivated in our talks in the days leading into the semi-final, and we believed that we had a shot at beating Kerry and getting to the final. So, why were lads also planning a big night out on the town?

I thought Croke Park would suit our running game.

I took my place amongst our subs in their area of the stand. It was a bitterly cold day, and as usual the shadow of the Hogan Stand added a few degrees of extra chill. The minute the game started, it struck me. From the very first minute. Kerry had moved up a gear from last time we had seen them. They were revving up for the championship.

Everything they did was twice as fast as they had played in our game against them in Killarney. They also saw mismatches all over the field, and decided to plunder those areas of the pitch. We were unaware of any of these same mismatches.

And, if they saw an opportunity, if they saw a one-on-one, they dispatched the ball long and with breathtaking accuracy.

They were ruthless.

They wanted goals, and seemed to have very little interest in kicking points. It was like they smelled blood, even though the game had just begun.

The game was over after 20 minutes.

Kieran Donaghy and David Moran were an enormous twin physical presence in the middle, and even though we kicked two of the first three points, they then put 1-5 on the board and made it look like child's play. The first goal also gave them a scent.

Colm Cooper scored the goal with that sweet left foot of his. Stephen O'Brien made it for him. A big delivery from Moran then found Donnachadh Walsh and he hammered it home. Darren O'Sullivan added their third before half-time.

Cooper had not played against us in Killarney. His presence made Kerry look twice as dangerous, and with him out there I had a sense that every time a chance came their way, they would make the right decision and they would execute it. Another team might have tapped one or two of their half-goal chances over the bar. Kerry were in a mood to take another pass, and another. They turned an easy point into an obvious goal.

We were two or three yards behind their forwards.

We were shadowing them, which meant they had a choice of looking to go by our defender or else hand pass the ball off. Either way, our defender was dead meat.

It was 3-8 to 0-5 at the break.

It ended 3-15 to 0-14.

Through it all, I had a bird's eye view of Eamonn Fitzmaurice at work for a second time in as many months. He was all coolness and total efficiency. It was like another day at the office for him. He was used to working in Croke

Park. And winning in Croke Park.

I was sitting there, and understanding that all my work in Croke Park up to this point was in the commentary booth far up in the sky above where I was now sitting. I thought I knew my way around Croke Park. I knew the layout of the place, sure, the dressing-rooms and the corridors and the people. I'd been 16 years walking around the place. I knew all of the different match day officials, all of them decent men. In the three hours before every match I'd spend time talking to most of them before doing my commentary.

But, I had none of Fitzmaurice's experience.

IT WAS CLEAR that our lads were nervous before the ball was even thrown up. They anticipated what was ahead of them.

A faster surface.

A flying football.

And the size of the place which makes it difficult for players to read distances. Croke Park does not look or feel like just another field when you are down there standing on that same field. It's harder to judge the flight of a long ball. It's harder to make a critical pass. Everything is different. And we did not handle any of it well. We got disconnected. There was no support running, or not half enough of it.

We lost their runners.

We had defenders left one-on-one all over the place.

And one piece of footage that I looked through, over and over again, in the days that followed showed Donaghy bringing one of our defenders for what appeared to be an aimless jog. He brought our man out of the centre and over to the Cusack Stand sideline.

There was a tangle of players.

Donaghy is next seen walking back onto the field, slowly enough, and making it back to his position in the centre of our defence... and there is nobody following him. The most dangerous player in Ireland possibly, and it looked like he had decided to go and sit down in the stand and then amble back out onto the field, without a single Roscommon footballer taking a blind bit of notice of him.

It was bizarre to watch it, and disturbing.

THEN AGAIN, I remember myself as a forward out in a smaller Croke Park. Back in the 80s. I remember getting an early ball and turning, and thinking of tapping it over the bar, and then thinking some more. I was uncertain how far out I was.

Where am I?

Distance is hard to calculate in Croke Park because of the massive surroundings and the fierce noise. 'Have Dublin an advantage playing there?' When people ask that question, they are buying into a foolhardiness and an innocence.

Dublin have a ten-fold advantage over every other team.

They know every inch of that field.

IT WAS DEMORALISING at half-time, having to give a team talk in the dressing-room and trying to paint any upside to what lay ahead.

Good teams, I know, are not beaten at half-time.

Teams that are managed well and prepared impeccably are not finished off halfway through a game. I was already blaming myself.

Did we pick the wrong team?

I already knew there were a couple of our lads who should not have been out there against Kerry. It was a level above them. It would always be a level above them. They did not have the mobility. They could play in Division Three and Division Two, and that was it. They were good footballers who were inferior athletes.

Neither were they able to think fast.

And me?

I would have to be brutally honest with myself, too.

It took too long for me to get there, however, and a couple of months later when we were kicked out of the championship by Clare in our round four qualifier I was still seeing Clare forwards taking on one or two of our defenders on the outside, and winning the race. Footballers from Clare whom I had barely heard of before I started preparing for the game were taking on our lads and they were full sure that they could win crucial foot races, on the inside or the outside.

It was heart-breaking to watch.

The Clare defeat would be as alarming to me as the Kerry defeat. We had defenders who were not able to shepherd Clare forwards towards the sideline. We had Clare forwards looking up and down at one or two of our defenders, and thinking they would have it easy once they got the ball.

There are two things in football you cannot coach, I resolved by the end of the summer. There is no coaching size, and there is no coaching real speed.

Explosiveness is exactly that.

It's a precious quality. Kerry had it when they cut through us in the league semi-final, and Clare had it in the championship when they brought our year to a close.

Kerry, especially, was demoralising. I could see their confidence spread out all over Croke Park, and they knew they were better foot passers than us, and they knew they were better hand passers than us, and they wanted us to see just how superior they really were. All of the deficits in our game were completely accentuated that day.

It was awful to watch.

I shook hands with Eamonn Fitzmaurice when it was all over, and I just wanted to get back on our team bus. I wanted to share what I was feeling with the whole team, even if we were not in the mood to say anything much to one another.

On our bus there was no team, however.

6

ROSCOMMON 1-15 NEW YORK 0-17
CONNACHT SFC PRELIMINARY ROUND
NEW YORK
MAY 2

I HAVE NO idea whether it was the basement of a church or a school, where we ended up a couple of hours or so after the game. We'd eaten first. The mood in the dressing-room was the absolute worst. I'd spoken for two or three minutes with them all. They'd mixed with some friends for 30, 40 minutes, and then we all got on the bus.

I was still fuming.

Actually, I was finding it hard to think straight.

I was confused and still panicked by the performance I had just seen. But I was also boiling with anger. Cian Connolly, a young lad from my own club, a corner-forward from the Gaels in Roscommon, had broken his jaw near the end. Whatever had happened to him, it had happened off the ball.

I sought out Maurice Deegan, the referee, before I went near our own dressing-room. I found him in a tiny little room at the back of the building.

'We've a fella in there,' I told him, '… and he's got a broken jaw!

'It's your job to make sure that does not happen!'

He apologised. He said he saw nothing.

'What about your linesmen?'

He said that if they saw something, they would have done something about it.

'And what am I supposed to tell his family?' I asked, thinking of Cian's father, who is a neighbour of mine, and a Garda Sergeant in the town.

'He's in my care... and what am I supposed to tell them? That nobody saw another man break his jaw?'

Thirty years earlier, I had my own jaw dislocated by a Galway opponent, who elbowed me and was later hit with a three-month suspension. You'd think that that sort of Wild West stuff was way in the past. But we were in New York City, in 2016, with five or six thousand people watching, and one man can break another man's jaw.

I knew the Connacht Council would do nothing about it when we got home.

And I was right.

WE'D ASKED OUR local liaison man in New York, Jimmy Naughton to find us somewhere quiet, where we could simply disappear from sight for a little while after the game. It wasn't to hide. I didn't want our lads getting dragged into pubs in the city quickly after the game, not at five o'clock. Afterwards would be fine.

That's why we ended up in a room with no windows.

My mistake.

It was a mess of a room. There were chairs thrown around the place and all I could think was... *this is like a feckin Quentin Tarantino movie!*

Everyone looked pissed off.

Some lads were sitting, but I chose to stand at the side of the room. I'd decided immediately after the game that we would go with Plan A. We'd get on the team bus, and just go. Get far away from Gaelic Park and McLean Avenue and The Bronx. I felt a need to purge ourselves, to face down what had just happened to us, but it was a mistake. It was a big mistake. It was not a good time to ask everyone to take accountability.

'This isn't good enough!'

'The money that was spent... and that's all we can do?'

'Did we get it wrong as a management... did we let you down?'

'All of the people who came over here... to look at us!'

'All the people we've let down!'

That's what the management team had to say for itself before we handed the room over to the players. It wasn't of much value in feeding the players' thoughts.

By then, the room looked even uglier than before.

Spirits were too low.

Everyone was raw.

The talk started slowly, but then, when it built up a head of steam, too many lads wanted to have their say or reply to someone who had just spilled out a home truth.

Too many lads got hot.

Too many were angry, and players started in on players. It was all pouring out. It was getting to the point where some lads were going to say something that they would never be able to take back.

I stood there, listening. I decided to let it wash through, but I let it go too far. But, still, I refused to call a stop. I've no idea what I was thinking.

Finally, Liam shouted... 'ENOUGH!'

I WAS STILL thinking of Cian Connolly.

I should have been with him, and not listening to our lads losing it with one another, and me standing there, doing nothing.

It was Liam McHale and David Casey who stepped in and took control.

I was so lost in my thoughts.

But I should have been with young Cian, wherever he was? I did not even know at that point whether he was already in a nearby hospital.

WE'D LEFT FOR New York on the Thursday.

There was a long, miserable Sunday evening ahead of us, and a Monday that seemed it would never end before we got on our flight for home, at last.

We'd put so much time and energy into the whole trip and we got nothing in return. We also gave nothing, and with Roscommon having such a huge footprint on the east coast of the United States that was simply unforgivable.

Fergal and I took on the brunt of the social engagements that filled the four nights, and we were careful in minimising the involvement of the players. It should have been an outstanding trip. We had no excuses.

Our hotel which was a good hour outside of Manhattan, our team room, our transport, everything was perfection. We didn't want the lads to tire themselves out traipsing around the city, looking at the sights and shopping, so we limited that time. It was warm from the Thursday evening, when we attended an early evening barbecue and then had a light run around the same field. On the Friday morning, we had a run-out in Gaelic Park. The pitch was far from a 4G surface.

It was more like a 1G, and on Sunday afternoon after the rain had been coming down all morning long, it was also slippery as hell.

The big event of the weekend had been listed for Rosie O'Grady's pub in the centre of Manhattan on Saturday, and the majority of the management team attended with a handful of players. It was jammers, but we were all back in our hotel by 11.0. We woke up to the rain lashing against our bedroom windows on Sunday morning.

It was a thoroughly filthy looking day.

We were favoured by 22 points with most bookmakers, but we never got going. We had named five championship debutantes. New York were keen, and very tight. Quickly enough, it became apparent that we were not going to get away from them.

I chose to stand and watch the game from one of the embankments, right in the middle of a few hundred spectators. It was the best vantage point I could find. It was also the hardest game of football I ever had to watch.

We were like the Keystone Cops.

Every single mistake we could possibly think of making, we were making out on the field. And there was no mistake too stupid, that we avoided making.

At half-time we did not manage to arrest anything, and in the second-half we got worse and worse, and worse. Senan Kilbride kicked the winning point from far out near the sideline, taking a shot he should never have considered in the first place. Thankfully, he did.

But they still had the winning of the game. They had a clear goal chance. I watched and, as if in slow motion, I waited for the shot to be taken. Either he got nervous, or he was too cocky, or both merged into one erring decision.

The New York forward delayed his shot. He tried to make doubly certain. He didn't let his shot off, and when he did the ball hit off the ankle of our goalkeeper and flew over the bar. They should have won the game. Deep into the second-half I was mostly trying to work out two things. First of all, I couldn't figure out what plans the GAA had for a team from Ireland who flew out to New York and lost in the preliminary round game? Did that team still get to play in the qualifiers?

I'd no idea. But, also, I was thinking that if we lost, would Fergal and I be resigning before we even got home? Or would we wait till we actually arrived back in Roscommon.

Definitely, we'd have to tender our resignations, I told myself. But, each time I came to this conclusion I also found myself wondering if the Roscommon board would ask the pair of us to remain on in our positions for the qualifying game.

If there was a qualifying game for us?

Maurice Deegan blew up the game about 40 seconds too early, by my reckoning. He saved our necks, though not on purpose.

THE ABSOLUTE MADNESS of the GAA fixtures calendar ensured that we'd had to race into our opening championship game, hot on the heels of losing the league semi-final. And then, we had a three weeks wait before meeting Leitrim in the opening round of the championship proper in Carrick-on-Shannon, and another three weeks wait for our semi-final against Sligo in Hyde Park.

We nailed the Leitrim game, 1-21 to 0-11. They finished with 12 men. We dominated every position on the field, and 10 different men contributed to our final tally. It was too easy to be either enjoyable or satisfying.

We needed to do the same with Sligo, and while we won 4-16 to 2-13, we failed to be even remotely business-like in our performance. As a group, we had told ourselves from the very start of the summer that teams like Leitrim and Sligo needed to be dealt with in the same manner as Mayo and Galway usually treated them. There should be no kerfuffle, no major or minor dramas. No question of any, but even though we had nine points to spare over Sligo we did not act or in any way perform as the 'New Roscommon' we talked about becoming which, bluntly, was a Roscommon team that set out to demoralise Leitrim and Sligo and not only win the game, but leave them with very little interest in seeing Roscommon again for quite some time.

That was the psyche we talked about creating within our group.

When we all sat down in my home as a management team in the week after coming home from New York we had looked at our shambolic performance and came to the conclusion that it was just that, a shambolic performance that did not offer us any insights or clues to where we actually stood at the beginning of the summer.

We did not have the stomach for the deep forensics.

We did not even recognise the team we had been working with for the previous six months, so where could we start? So, therefore, we started sifting through the performance but we never finished our body of work, not properly. If we had, we would have looked through New York and beyond. We would have gone back to the defeat by Kerry.

And we would have gone back to our terribly disappointing display against Mayo, and we would have joined all of the dots and we would have seen that we were slowly falling off the cliff edge.

We opted, instead, to sign off on New York as a blip.

The single major positive, amongst many minor positives, in the win over Leitrim was that we set about becoming far more aggressive on their kick-outs, and we pushed up high at all times. Leitrim were forced to kick too many balls long and when they did we flooded the middle. We swept up everything. We did the same again against Sligo.

But, there was a problem.

AS PLAIN AS the nose on my face, I could see that not all of our forwards had the athleticism to really push up hard all the time. Some of them were not even very good at doing it some of the time.

It should be a simple procedure.

If you want the opposition to push a kick out to the right, then the two men in the full-forward line simply split. They are the only two there, because the third has already made it out to the middle to claim loose ball in case of a long kick. All we had to do was split, and invite their goalkeeper to kick the ball to the right corner-back. Still simple enough?

We wanted the ball to go to their right corner-back, because we had concluded that he is their weakest ball player. We'd have watched him for weeks, and we knew that he would take off up the line. He'd do that, because we would give him just enough room and sufficient incentive to do so.

Still simple!

No great science at work. We do not want to pressurise him too quickly. We want him to believe he's got time and room to solo and look further down the field. Then, we want to collapse in on him. Make him see he's got no more room.

Make him panic.

We pressure him and, because he is their weakest man on the ball in their own defence, he'll likely make a mistake and give the ball up. That's how it is supposed to work, right from the beginning, when our full-forward line splits and makes it obvious to their goalkeeper where he must dink the ball.

Once we entice the goalkeeper and he does what we want him to do, then our two full-forwards chase across the field and hunt down the corner-back with the ball. At that stage they don't give a damn about the unmarked corner-back they are leaving behind. It's up to us to cast the net. Get there fast, and see to it that the sideline is used as an extra set of Roscommon forwards.

Problem was, not all of our forwards could cover the ground fast enough once the kick-out was taken.

IT HAS TO be that simple.

However, if one man is not doing his job, then the other team can play 'Overlap City'. If both of our full-forwards did not make the 30 metres sprint, every single time, we're just giving them free passage out of their defence.

Donie Shine did not make our squad for the following season, basically because he lacked the speed that is demanded in the modern game, in our estimation. That is why one of Roscommon's most outrageously gifted forwards of modern times was getting a phone call from me telling him that his county career was about to come to a premature end.

It still was not an easy call.

Donie was a big brand footballer, not only in Roscommon. Everyone in the country knew of him as a man with a thundering belt of a ball, and someone with uncommon accuracy for such a big man. Donie was also a 'big man' as he listened to my explanation during our phone call.

We had an honest chat. He accepted what I had to say him, and very quickly his decade-long career with Roscommon came to a close. That was just one of a number of tough phone calls I had to make at the end of 2016. I made a big mistake in not taking on board David Keenan's huge disappointment.

I should have kept David on the squad instead of sticking to my decision, and two days later the error of my ways was magnified. One of the lads I had kept on the panel called and told me he would be unavailable for 2017. There was an opening for David. But I should not have needed an opening. I should have listened.

I knew David Keenan was one of the hardest working and most committed footballers any manager could find, and I knew he would be an addition to most county panels. I just doubted his overall football ability, and wrongly so. I phoned him and apologised, and admitted my error. He thought about it, but I realised that I had genuinely hurt him.

He wanted to play for Roscommon more than any other man, probably. But he turned down my invitation.

We had decided that we would only bring 28 players into squad training for 2017, which meant trimming numbers by eight men. The county board accounts were not good, and we needed to save money. We had overspent. The board needed tighter numbers, but thinking we could get away with 28 was also an error. I pared things back, but pretty soon into 2017 we were back in the low thirties again.

OUR VICTORY OVER Sligo was a model in how to win a game out of mayhem. It was a game characterised by chaos and while we kept our heads after finding ourselves eight points down in the first-half we could not take any pride out of the afternoon. The two goals we gave away were infantile, fourth class national school defending.

There was a massive wind working its way down the field, from head to toe. Within the chaos, interestingly, there was calmness amongst the lads out there. I could sense that, and because they were clear-headed we were able to take full advantage of two lucky breaks either side of half-time. Before the break they lost Adrian Marren to a black card, and he had been causing us lots of trouble in our full-back line. Twenty seconds into the second-half Senan Kilbride pounced for a goal. That was enough for us to be convinced that we had the winning of the game, and Senan fisting Niall Daly's big high delivery to the back of the net also showed us that Sligo were not too sure about their sizeable lead.

Ciaráin Murtagh got the equalising goal in the 49th minute. With 20 minutes remaining he put us one point up, and one minute later he drove a penalty to the net after Senan was fouled. David Keenan, playing in an auxiliary central role in the middle of the field, kicked three points but not enough, unfortunately, to rid me of my foolish doubts about him.

We had played four matches over two and a half months, and we had a Connacht final against Galway now in our sights, but we had no momentum.

That was the over-riding sensation.

It was like we were all half-waiting to see how the season might finally turn out.

7

ROSCOMMON 1-10 GALWAY 0-13
CONNACHT SFC FINAL
GALWAY
JULY 10

QUICKLY ENOUGH, IT was obvious to me that we were becoming one of those tight, defensive teams which was preoccupied with building all sorts of high and low walls in their own half of the field. Thing is, I'd no idea how we became one of those teams.

It was not my desire for us to think and breathe defensively.

I wanted a fluidity, and I wanted us to be an ambitious team who believed in moving the ball quickly out of defence alright, but principally a team that did not buy into a strong sense of its own mortality.

Every team out there was terrified of dying.

And why?

Ninety-nine per cent of teams die every season, at some point, before one team gets to be crowned top dog.

What is there to be afraid of?

That was my thinking. Let us not be afraid. So, where was the Roscommon team I was trying to build all those months?

WE WOKE UP, the morning of our trip to Pearse Stadium, and it was another ferociously wet day in the making. It was perfectly horrible, even looking out at it. And we had to try to play in a Connacht final, in Salthill of all places in Ireland, on a day like that?

We travelled.

But there was no question of seeking to conquer anyone. In fact, neither team in the final looked like they were all that bothered about boldly winning the game. The whole afternoon took on this surreal tactical battle.

I've no real sense, still, of how it came about.

Certainly I did not tell our lads to fall back and stay back. The game from the very start was one great pile of logjams.

It was nuts to watch. I had not expected this from Galway.

I hadn't expected it from us! We had been building and working so hard for several months on being stronger defensively and, to me, it appeared as though our whole team almost became mesmerised, if not hypnotised, watching what Galway were at in their half of the field. The two teams ended up becoming a mirror image of one another.

I didn't like it.

We did not have enough fat on the scoreboard and, in effect, we had bought into a game that would be decided most probably in the final 10 minutes, and most likely by one ingenious play by one player or one piece of outrageous luck. It was no way to win or lose a Connacht final in my book.

We needed to take on Galway.

Roscommon had met Galway five times in the Connacht championship since 2001 and had lost all five. The average loss was 10 points, and in a tight finish Galway would expect to win again. Also, but of equal importance, why should younger Roscommon footballers who were not party to those defeats accept a fate which was either to get lucky or sneak a victory. These same footballers were under-21 Connacht champs in three of the previous five years. Some of them had enjoyed three wins in the last four meetings between the counties at minor level.

And, still, the 2016 Connacht final went to the plan of Galway and the Gods.

We had to rely on a free-kick from Donie Smith in the third minute of added time to make it a draw and make certain of getting a second chance.

It was a tough kick, and into the teeth of a terrible wind. 'You'll never have nerves again… ever,' I told him, 'taking a pressurised free!' And, indeed, 12 months later he kicked an impossible free-kick in Croke Park and one that he had no right to score, which landed on the top of the Mayo net to earn us another replay.

But, in Salthill, we should have won the Connacht title.

After Smith's equaliser, we won the ball back and we had John McManus, one of our most forceful runners on the ball, and he was tearing out of our defence and, just as he was about to be hit late by a Galway man, he passed the ball off.

Deep in injury-time there was a sense of madness to the game, total chaos out there on the field, with nobody marking up anymore, and the ball was about to be worked down the field. And it was going to certainly end with us easily finding a man who would have nobody near him, and have an easy shot for the winning point of the game.

But, no.

Conor Lane, the referee, blew his whistle. He took out his black card. Galway were down to 14 men, but they suddenly had all of those 14 men behind the ball. We had possession and we played it over and back in front of their 45 metres line, but there was no room, no opening developing and the final whistle was blown with the ball in our hands.

I HATED HOW we had played.

We spent a whole Connacht final fluting around in our own half of the field.

'Can you not be positive?

'Push… UP!' I told them at half-time.

It was crazy carry-on, but it was like nobody was listening to me. They were winning by two points as the game reached 70 minutes, and we needed all the bravery of Cathal Cregg and then Donie Smith to save our necks. His brother, Enda's first-half goal had given us a 1-6 to 0-6 advantage at the break, but we proceeded to live off the back of that goal for far too long. We earned a replay.

But that was not what we set out to do that morning.

We did not go to Pearse Stadium to reach a standstill. Hyde Park was out of commission for the replay, but we as a management team refused to return to Salthill.

We were all heading to Castlebar.

REPLAYS CAN BE headstrong.

They have a mind of their own, often enough, and they can be stubborn enough to disconnect themselves from the game that came before.

Thirty-one years earlier, I had been in one of the most famous drawn games and replays of the 1980s. It was Mayo and Dublin, and the 1985 All-Ireland final awaited one of us. It was a summer of Bruce Springsteen in Slane, and moving statues in every second village in Ireland, and they dominated the news. But the Mayo team that Liam O'Neill managed also got everyone's attention.

We'd gone to Hyde Park and we'd demolished Roscommon to win in Connacht, and finish off that great team which was brilliantly led by Dermot Earley. I kicked a bagful of points from frees in the first-half and we led 1-9 to 0-1 at the break. They were 1/8 on in pre-match odds with the bookmakers, and it would be Dermot's final game in the primrose and blue. We came to Croke Park to meet Dublin seriously believing in ourselves, but between the drawn game and the replay something happened to the team's massive confidence.

That Mayo team was also hungry.

Mayo had won no Connacht title in the 1970s, and in the late 70s and early 80s it was all about Roscommon. But we had a lot of the 1983 All-Ireland under-21 winning team pouring into the senior dressing-room. There must have been four or five of us on the team, all seriously talented footballers like John Maughan and John Finn, Peter Forde and Noel Durkan, and there were another four or five on the subs bench. I was in UCG with Maughan, and we'd travel up and down to training together and the talk all the time between us was that this is 'beyond a joke... we have to win something!'

In the 1983 Connacht final we should have beaten Galway, but we ran out of steam, and the following year we made some catastrophic errors in the final. Again it was Galway. There was no back door in those days. We got one fierce bad call against us, when the referee Mickey Kearns cancelled out a goal for 'square ball' when the man in question, Big Tom Byrne had barely tip-toed into the large rectangle.

I was thin as a whippet, and even fitter, as I was just out of the cadets. But I was also capable of acting the maggot and avoiding any hard slog in training. O'Neill decided he needed a personal trainer on my case, on site in Galway, and he got Brendan Hutchinson from Galway athletics circles on board. He would meet me on site.

And Maughan, who was a fitness fanatic, would also turn up for the extra work. He never missed squad training, but he didn't want to miss additional sessions. Tom Carr would also appear. Whether I liked it or not, I was in the shape of my young life.

Sean Lowry was a true leader with that Mayo team. He'd won two All-Irelands with Offaly and he was closing down his career, but he wanted a little more. I found him a calming influence, too, as I ended up travelling a fair bit with him.

'You're a bloody good player!' he'd tell me.

'The lads in Offaly... they're not half as good as you!'

Whether he believed this or not, he liked to stoke my confidence with his words. It helped that he was in full-forward, and that I was in the corner next to him. He broke a clatter of ball down for me, and if anyone acted the pup with me he'd also see to it that they'd think again about messing with me a second time.

I also had Micheal O'Muircheartaigh in my corner. The legendary RTE commentator was training the Kerry lads in Dublin for Mick O'Dwyer, and the rest of us were always invited to join in, so I was marking Mick Spillane in six-a-side games and I was beating him often enough.

This fella's winning All-Irelands every September!

Me telling myself that, and Sean Lowry telling me good things, had me believing I would help Mayo to beat Dublin in the All-Ireland semi-final. Micheal was great. He was not cutting edge when it came to training. Any Mayo lad who spent a week up in Dublin and joined us would go back down home and tell everyone... 'They're doing nothing up there... only football, football, football!'

True. Though we also had a mile run at the start of every evening. Jack O'Shea won every single one of them, despite the fact that Dermot Flanagan would burst a gut to get close to him. The rest of us would be a lap down on the pair of them.

We knew the Kerry lads and felt comfortable in their company, and Kerry had beaten Dublin fairly comprehensively in the 1984 All-Ireland final, and would do so again in '85, as it turned out. Because of that, we had no fear of Dublin in our first semi-final.

We got off to a shocking start, but for the rest of the game I was scoring heavily and it was this game in which I was voted Man of the Match, more than anything else, that cemented my All-Star award. I marked Dave Synott the first day but Kevin Heffernan didn't let me have it as easy in the replay, and dispatched the late Mick Holden to put some manners on me and he did so, mostly legitimately because of his amazingly wise head.

The first day John Finn had his jaw broken. The controversy over that was one item that helped to dismantle us as a team between the two games.

There would be other things, too.

We went on the lash the night of the first game, of course. There was also a fairly big row before the night got really going when a few of us were sitting on the bus, waiting for everyone to leave the Ashling Hotel around the corner from Heuston Station and head for home. But lads inside would not come out. Sean Lowry and his wife, Nuala wanted to go. They had children at home, and they probably had a babysitter, but there was no moving the lads inside and in the end they only came out nearly an hour later under protest.

We should have been gone by 6.30 pm. It was 8.30 pm when we got going, but only when agreement was reached that the bus would stop at The Beaten Path, which is outside Claremorris. Sean had to get a lift home to Crossmolina from there.

It was pure madness.

For all we knew, we would be meeting Dublin again seven days later. In the end, the game was put further back, but nobody really cared when it was going to be played as we marched into The Path, which had an arched entrance on it that was the spitting image of the welcome to Pablo Escobar's ranch in Colombia.

The pub also had the biggest nightclub in the country. That's where we stayed till daybreak, and that is where we also slept. Most of us.

We were back!

That was the Mayo psyche back then, and it was agreed that no matter what happened in the replay nobody could take that away from us. *We're back!* There were big crowds at training. The buzz was unreal, and then we got well beaten by Dublin in the replay, fools that we were.

CONCERTED EFFORTS TO get things right between the two games came undone, like when we sat down for our first review meeting and Liam O'Neill determinedly put a VHS tape into the recorder. We were back in The Beaten Path for that meeting, appropriately enough.

He moved through the different stages of the game and there were many crucial events, but one moment dominated our entire meeting. There was a small TV at the top of the room, and we arrived at the moment in the second-half when Pádraig Brogan, the young hotshot of Mayo football, was introduced into the game by Liam. The video tape showed Liam on the sideline with his arm around Brogan, talking into his ear.

'Do you remember what I was saying, Pádraig?' Liam asked.

We could see Liam handing Brogan the slip of paper.

There was 15 minutes to go in the game.

The game was on a knife edge.

'Pádraig!' Liam continued. 'I told you to go to midfield, and to move TJ (Kilgallon) to No.11 and tell Willie Joe to go into No.14.'

Brogan piped up in the room. 'Yeah, that's right!' he stated.

'It's the most critical stage of the match,' stated Liam, '... and we're back in it, and I am making a big substitution! Now... run the tape, and see what happens next!'

We all look at Pádraig Brogan striding onto the field, and handing the slip of paper to the match referee, John Moloney and, then... Brogan takes off!

He talks to nobody.

There is total confusion on the field.

'Does everyone see what Pádraig did?' asked Liam.

The whole room erupted into laughter. I joined in. But someone else did not, and Dermot Flanagan got a water bottle that was parked at his feet and he threw it back down onto the ground.

Dermot was the only man in Mayo, in the 80s, who would have a water bottle. But he was also one thousand per cent correct to react like he did.

'FUCK THIS!' he shouted and took on the room. We all understood, at that stage, that we had only been laughing at ourselves. But the biggest elephant in our camp between the two games was the Sean Lowry Affair.

Liam O'Neill was coming under pressure to drop Sean, bowing to a belief amongst Mayo supporters that if a forward is not scoring then he is not contributing. After a game in those days when there was a lot less TV analysis, and no social media breakdown of games, people looked at the scorers in their newspapers and reached judgment.

Sean had not been scoring, but he was getting the ball to me and I was scoring, or else he was getting fouled and I was popping those free-kicks over the bar. Dropping Sean Lowry was a disastrous decision. The whole atmosphere in the dressing-room changed at that moment and, in addition, Sean was not around.

We did not see him again, until he arrived at the Marine Hotel in Sutton the day of the game. We all had been up the night before and asking ourselves would we see him?

Personally, I was devastated not to have him out there.

Sean had that confidence, and also that cuteness, and he had been on Offaly teams that had beaten Dublin often enough and did not view them as being anything special. As I said, he was a true leader and believer in our camp.

He nearly tore the netting off the rigging when he smashed the ball home in the Connacht final against Roscommon, and he had told us before the game to expect that exact moment. We were all a little nervy in the old dressing-rooms in Roscommon, which had been built a hundred yards from the field, when Sean stood up and gave one of his great speeches.

'Do ye realise the talent ye have in here, in this room?' he began. 'Will ye stop making excuses... bending the knee!

'Let it flow out there... GO FOR IT!

'And, at some stage, I will get a chance and... I will... BURY IT!

'When that happens, I'll look around and I'll put my finger in the air and... when I put my finger in the air, we're heading for home lads!'

You could really take your pick and list, in order of severity, which events caused the Mayo team most damage between those two games back in 1985.

Me? I'd have the dropping of Sean Lowry No.1.

IN THE CONNACHT final replay, in 2016, Galway won their 45th provincial title and they did so with considerable ease. They won it in the opening 35 minutes.

It was one of those games that was over and gone by half-time. From the beginning, Tom Flynn and Paul Conroy started winning a giant share of clean ball in the middle third, and they were enjoying plentiful possession and, this time, Kevin Walsh had evidently told them to tear into us without any fear. They did so.

Shane Walsh and Danny Cummins ran fearlessly at us, and Damien Comer was eating up the ball when it came anywhere near him. To say we were surprised was an understatement. We as a management team had not prepared the lads right, and the lads did not respond when they found themselves being overrun.

It finished 3-16 to 0-14.

We had David Keenan dropping back deep and looking to serve as a sweeper, but with Galway as happy to run with the ball as kick it inside, he was unable to carry out his duties as we had all imagined. In the third, fourth and fifth minutes they had three points, and Cummins' first goal on 20 minutes killed off the game as a contest. A poor kick out from us helped Gary Sice to score their second three minutes later, and it was 2-9 to 0-5 at half-time, and on a dry, and nicely warm afternoon that was perfect for good football, there was no catching them.

IN THE HOURS after the defeat, and even the days, we did not know where we were as a group. We had not played really well in months, and only our win over Leitrim had fed us anything positive about ourselves.

We were a group of men riddled with doubts.

And that included all of the management team, as we asked ourselves…
What have we achieved this season?

Have we actually built a team here… at all?

We felt we were in Nowhere Land.

Six days later, we were due to meet Clare in a round four qualifying match in Pearse Stadium. And there was a huge prize a little further down the road, an All-Ireland championship quarter-final against Kerry back in Croke Park.

Kerry again? Meeting them was a prize that once thrilled us but, in late July, we did not even raise our heads to view that same prize. Every single day there were the same doubts. Same questions.

Who's good enough?

Who wants it?

So, we decided that even though we were getting late into the season we'd look afresh at every single man and decide on every man individually.

8

CLARE 2-12 ROSCOMMON 1-9
ALL-IRELAND QUALIFIERS ROUND 4
GALWAY
JULY 24

WE DECIDED UPON an honest, winner-takes-all game of A Vs B.

That game, on the Wednesday evening, was the only run-out we had the whole week as we stewed and waited to see. We were desperate, guilty of tugging at hope. 'Give it everything you all have...' the lads were informed.

'And we'll pick the men who want it most!'

That's what we said, and then we went and picked the team to play against Clare and we did the exact opposite. We were not true to our word. If we were, at least four men would not have started against Clare.

Four others had shown us, beyond any doubt, that they had a greater want.

CLARE WERE ROCK solid at the back. Even when they went down to 14 men after a straight red card was shown to Cathal O'Connor just after half-time, the flow of the game was not at all altered. The numbers were evened up later in the half when Sean Mullooly got two yellows. Didn't matter, Clare hadn't flinched.

They scored two goals in the first-half and won by six points in the end, on a 2-12 to 1-9 scoreline. The damage was really done two days earlier when all of us, the five selectors, took a full day and met in Boyle to choose our team. We met in Fergal's house, starting about lunchtime.

On the way to Boyle, I had received a phone call from Liam, who unburdened himself of his mounting frustrations. He felt he was being sidelined by the rest of the management team as the season had gathered up steam, and he admitted to me that he did not even know why he was bothering to show up at selection meetings anymore.

I sought to calm him.

'We don't need to talk about this today,' I cautioned him. 'Let's get through this, and see where we are by the end of the week, okay?'

He agreed, but warned me that he would not be part of the management team in 2017. 'I don't believe what we're doing as a group is right!' he stated bluntly. 'I haven't believed in what we're doing for a long time.'

I honestly had so many doubts. I was weighing up everything and while I knew that we were not utilising Liam fully, I was bothered by so many questions that I had not resolved myself, like… *Is coaching art, or science?*

Or is it horse whispering?

Is there too much coaching, too much talking about tactics and match-ups and…

Are we smothering ourselves with a mixture of truths and nonsense?

Liam then told me that he had a team in his head that would be able to beat Clare. He had coached Clare, and he knew them better than anyone. 'We put out that same team, that we did last week… and we'll get the run around from these lads on Saturday,' he insisted.

I tried to play down his prediction.

'They're small,' he added. 'But, they're flyers!'

'They've seen us… and Colm Collins, I'm telling you, he believes they can beat us… if we don't surprise him.'

We finished up, after he had one last request. 'When we get into this meeting, remember, this is the team I want to see us select.'

He then named out his team to me.

I had one or two different players to him, but I kept his words in my head and his firm belief that we needed men out there who had serious legs, and who could run.

The selection meeting lasted five hours.

We were around a kitchen table and nobody kept an eye on the time. That was a feature of how we had worked as a management team all season. We put in as many hours as were needed, and we spent far too long at it. Fergal and I always had the final say on selection, but with five people around a table, and five sets of opinions on every single player, there are inevitably trade-offs and compromises. Which is not the best thing.

Liam, and Stephen and David, left. And Fergal and I shared one final pot of tea. I told him I was not mad about the team we'd selected, and he returned his thoughts. We both agreed we were still good enough to win and get through to the All-Ireland quarter-final.

Back in my car and about five miles down the road, I got a call from Liam who was making his longer journey back to Ballina, and he was still agitated.

'You realise the team we've just picked,' he said, '… you know it has eight lads on it who are different to the team I called out to you on my way down to the meeting.

'Did you hear the warnings I gave you about Clare's pace?'

He did not look for an answer, and told me he'd leave it at that, that we'd both had a long and tough day, but before hanging up he could not stop himself from adding…

'We're just picking the wrong players!'

I SAW THE resignation statement released by Fergal O'Donnell, and Stephen Bohan and David Casey, on my computer screen before it hit the newspapers or social media. I received it directly from the county board. And I found it deeply disappointing. The statement would split support for me in the county, and would end up making my subsequent two years extra difficult.

Also, I did not agree with everything in it.

It was a long and deeply personal statement from the hearts of men who absolutely care about the good of Roscommon football, and it would be wrong for me to present portions of it here and now, or analyse what they said. The people of Roscommon had the opportunity to read the statement in full, and decide for themselves on its content. Neither will I present the 12 page season review that I wrote for the county board and which discussed our strengths and weaknesses as a management team.

But, I feel it would be remiss of me not to share my synopsis of how we had worked as a management team, which I presented in three paragraphs. Unlike the other statement, this review has never seen the light of day publicly.

A: I believe myself and Fergal enjoyed excellent personal relationships throughout the 2016 season and this helped to provide cohesion and focus for the squad and backroom team. We both worked very hard over the nine-months long season (Nov 2015-July 2016) but during championship some differences in philosophy regarding management style, playing style, panel selection and in particular team selection and administrative decisions led I believe to a sense of frustration among all members of the management team.

B: By the end of the season, I believed that we both realised that our management structure and backroom team was in need of changes and freshening up. Ultimately, I concluded that joint management had not worked out to my satisfaction and was unlikely to work in the future. We are both strong personalities but in the interest of cohesion and a united front, I very much took a background position in the early days of the season. Later in the season, especially in the area of team selection and tactical approach, I did end up frustrated with the process.

C: I believe we ultimately failed to provide the positive environment and coaching philosophy that might provide for championship success. By summer's end we had once again failed to enjoy a successful championship, our playing form had dipped dramatically, our management team was somewhat fractured and the failure to reach the AIQF was extremely disappointing.

In the remainder of my review I broke down the season, in greater detail, in which we had played 22 games, won 12, drawn one, and lost nine, and in which we had trialled 60 players, of whom 10 played in their first Connacht senior football final.

This book has not been written in order to claim that I was right and Fergal was wrong, or different shades of such views. I respect Fergal O'Donnell more than enough to know that he would only do what he felt was the right thing to do.

Similarly, I decided it was right for me to continue as sole manager of the Roscommon team, and by the end of October the Roscommon Board gave me their blessing to work in the job for another two years. I gratefully accepted.

However, if I had any sense that Fergal wished to take up the job on his own, I would have immediately stepped out of his way. And I told him this. I still believed I could make a difference and make the team better by taking up the manager's role on my own, but if Fergal wanted it I would have accepted that.

As I have already said, he was born in the county, and he is a giant in the eyes of everyone in the county. He is loved by the people of Roscommon.

I could never win a similar place in their hearts, and I did not set out into 2017 in order to do so. That was not on page one of my list of priorities. Besides, the statement from Fergal and the two lads would ensure only conditional support within the county during my tenure.

In 2017, I worked harder than I had ever worked at anything ever before in my life. I thought I could build a better working environment for everybody associated with the county team, and I thought we could win a Connacht title. I felt all through the season that I was under the ultimate spotlight.

I felt for long periods that there was a greater number of people waiting for me to fail, than the number wishing me to succeed. I often looked into the faces of my best friends or considered their opinions, and I was convinced they all thought I would not make it halfway through the 2017 season.

It was a tough year personally.

And it was the greatest year of my life as a manager, too.

There were times when I thought I might indeed crack, when results were bad and simply getting worse, but I never thought of resigning. Honestly.

The whole season, I felt that I had taken a bomb into my hands. It felt, without being overly dramatic, like a never-ending scene from the Oscar winning movie, *Hurt Locker* in which Jeremy Renner plays a specialist stationed in Iraq who is in the business of dismantling explosives.

Every day in 2017 was a pressure I had never known before.

But it was my decision to walk into 2017.

It was my choice.

2017

9

TYRONE 0-18 ROSCOMMON 1-9
NFL DIVISION ONE (ROUND 1)
OMAGH
FEBRUARY 5

I HAVE NO idea whether Jim Gavin, and men like him managing the best counties, have to lock up the gates at the end of a training night. But I doubt it, don't you? I also doubt they have to take out their own credit card and pay team bills.

The 2017 season gave me plenty of thumping headaches, and my stomach was in knots lots of the time, too. But there were other pressures. Events that slapped me in the face and left me seriously questioning what on earth was going on?

Like the Sunday evening we all boarded our team bus outside our hotel in Omagh, after losing to Mickey Harte and his expertly prepared team in our opening league game, and I saw Sean Finnegan, our logistics officer get on board last, and approach me with a pained expression on his face. My best friend did not have good news for me.

At the county board convention two months earlier, in December, our treasurer had admitted to delegates that the amount of money owed to creditors at the end of 2016 remained a 'major problem'. Seamus Maher, who is also a good friend of mine, was quizzed about many things at the meeting, including the costs of the Club Rossie bus. He replied that there were still 50 'large' monthly repayments that had to be made against the cost of the magnificent bus but that the Board was conscious of keeping costs as tight as possible, and that the bus was operated by volunteer drivers as a result of this. Truth is, by the close of 2016 the county board purse was empty.

I was sitting on the bus when Sean told me there was a problem with the hotel. They were not happy. The county board credit card was unable to cover the full costs of our 24 hours stay, and the hotel was not at all interested in waving the Roscommon team off and waiting for payment a week or two later.

Jesus Christ!

Fuck Sake!

A few months down the road, as we were leaving Fota Island in County Cork after a long training weekend, Sean came to me a second time.

I was able to cover both bills, and the team was able to depart, but only because of the gratuity I had received after retiring from the army. I had money there, in case someone in my family got sick, or there was an emergency.

Being manager of Roscommon, however, meant that the county team was family. On a number of occasions I also bought year-long gym membership for some of the players because the Board did not have access to money on a particular week. Things like this, like purchasing extra tickets for players, for instance, were a recurring theme during my three years.

I couldn't have a player waiting for a month to start a gym programme. Each time, I was repaid by the Board, and Seamus was always apologetic and thankful.

I KNEW HARTE from his earliest days in management.

Mickey Harte and I actually battled for the first time in the 2001 All-Ireland under-21 final when they beat us 0-13 to 0-10 in a game that was played in October. It was a final that we had to wait six months for, because we'd beaten Meath in the semi-final way back in April. At one point, Tyrone were told that they would have to exit the competition.

The Foot and Mouth crisis had caused mayhem to the GAA's fixtures programme. It was a long, confusing season.

One that also included me receiving a long letter from Mickey Harte, in which he threw himself at my feet, but also made it known that Mayo would not feel like 'true champions' unless my team had beaten his on the field of play. He put it to me that we both needed to find out who was 'the best team in Ireland'.

That was fine by me, too, and I didn't argue with Paraic Duffy when he called me in late April and asked me to agree to a postponement of our proposed All-Ireland final against Cork. Everyone was prepared to wait for Tyrone to play Cork in their 'semi' first. Except, a lot changed during the course of that summer.

For starters, all of Harte's team got serious senior championship experience. Six of them came through in Ulster, the likes of Cormac McAnallen, Conor Gormley, Stephen O'Neill, Brian McGuigan, Kevin Hughes and Owen Mulligan, and by the time we met them in October they had grown into more certain footballers than they would have been in the spring.

In the spring, also, Mayo had come off a National League victory and my lads, the likes of David Clarke, Alan Dillon, and Conor and Trevor Mortimer who were part of that experience were full of confidence. We would have taken Tyrone in the spring, I have no doubt about that, because we had already beaten them in the final of the Hastings Cup, in March, by a point in a game that went to extra-time.

That same summer I had to go to the Lebanon, and my team was disbanded. We were told that Cork and Tyrone would play one another at the earliest opportunity. That game was played two weeks before the final, whereas we had no competitive game for six months. Also, my Dad died just before the final against Tyrone.

He was my mentor and the team's kit man, and we buried him the day before the final.

WE'D LOST TO Galway in the FBD league final, in Kiltoom, at the end of January and that grated with me. We wanted to be chasing down Mayo in Connacht, and instead we were in danger of making losing to Galway something of a routine. I was also annoyed by all of our turnovers in the game.

We were together for over a year, and we were still turning over far too much ball to the opposition and forcing ourselves to work twice as hard in games.

Even though we got to the FBD final, we'd also lost to Mayo in January and it was an extra annoying loss. We'd been up by four or five points close to the finish and they grabbed two late goals. We'd beaten Mayo in the 2016 FBD and to have taken them again would have been fantastic. It might have told us something. Instead, their goals came in injury time and they sucked up the victory before our supporters in Kiltoom.

Andy Moran came off the field kissing the Mayo crest on his shirt. He'd scored the two late goals that sunk us.

There was a lot of pushing at the gate, as players left the field, as a result of this and while I was encouraged watching Mayo take so much satisfaction from beating us, in a fairly meaningless game in January, I would rather have won. But still, they obviously saw us as something of a danger to them in the short-to-medium term.

We lost to Mayo, 4-11 to 2-16.

We lost to Galway, 2-14 to 0-15.

We'd played well in both games, but there were two losses at our backs to our biggest neighbours and we had a league campaign about to start. And, consciously, very definitely after watching the team fall over the cliff edge midway through the previous season, I had decided to do far less work with our lads in preparation for the league campaign. I knew it was going to be very tough, and I had forewarned the county board that staying put in Division One could not be placed as a priority over Roscommon having a serious championship campaign.

It had to be championship first in 2017.

THERE'S NOTHING NICE about losing, however, even when you half expect it. And we had a lot of losing to do in the months of February and March.

Travelling up to Omagh was daunting.

It's a place where we have all seen Harte and his teams play some serious football in front of their own supporters. Tyrone, also, take the league seriously. At the same time, it was thrilling to be going to play in a ground that has grown into something of a fortress and that is now a testing 'experience' for every team who plays Tyrone there. It's like a football team in England going to Old Trafford or Anfield.

Games in Omagh matter, and I had the lads primed to play from the very first minute. Niall Daly scored an early goal, and we could have had two more but Mickey O'Neill made good saves from Ciaráin Murtagh and Ultan Harney. But, as only they can, Tyrone then hit their stride, which meant every single man in a white shirt hit the same stride at the exact same time. We didn't score for 17 minutes. It was 0-10 to 1-2 at half-time. It was foggy and chilly, and they had a tight hold on the game.

Game over, in truth, especially up there.

Despite the loss, and despite the pain in the ass of having to pay the team's hotel bill, Omagh was memorable for me. Getting to go head-to-head once again with Harte, for starters, was an honour. He stands on the sideline as the game's High Priest, someone whom everyone respects. He has done for Tyrone what every county dreams of doing. He brought his own county up by their boot-straps. It's not like Dublin and Kerry teams, who feed on the rich tradition and example of teams before them. Tyrone have done it from nothing, virtually. Harte, single-handedly, made it happen.

I don't agree with everything he has said and done, but I do admire him as a football boss. He was civil and quietly welcoming to me and the team before the game. All of the Tyrone officers were equally disarming in saying hello to us all.

The evening before the game they let us in for a kickabout. They made no fuss. They also thanked us for actually staying in the town. Evidently, not many teams chose to stay overnight in Omagh itself. On our way back home I kept thinking through how they had worn us down so swiftly in the first-half. It wasn't like it took them 40 or 50 minutes to get the job done. They had Tiernan McCann bombing, Colm Cavanagh dropping back in front of their D, and they had everyone else in such an impressive athletic state for so early in the year. But, how did we not have someone tracking Peter Harte as he came off the shoulder and as he made those long penetrating runs of his up the centre?

How do you stop Tyrone from being Tyrone?

We should have got our three early goals, however, and if we had then McCann and the others... *They would not have been so adventurous, would they?*

We'd looked to keep the game really tight.

But the goals, and the pivotal free we also missed, hurt us. We were only two or three points down when Fintan Cregg missed with that free. I was thinking, as we continued to travel south, about another moment in the game that really summed up who we are as a team, and who Tyrone are!

A Tyrone attack had broken down, and one of our best lads, Niall Kilroy had a great overlap and we had two men up on them. Niall was tearing down the wing, and all he had to do was make the correct pass back into the middle, to one of our big runners.

Niall put the ball behind our man and Tyrone picked up possession. That was the difference. Tyrone would never have messed up that pass.

Their passing is too good.

Ours was not good enough. A simple difference, but a huge difference between two teams. It can leave teams worlds apart. But I still felt good travelling home. We had shown fighting spirit to the very end. We gave a decent account of ourselves, and we did aswell as most other teams from the south have done in Omagh.

10

DONEGAL 0-16 ROSCOMMON 2-9
NFL DIVISION ONE (ROUND 2)
ROSCOMMON
FEBRUARY 12

CAREERS ARE INTERRUPTED, or ended, and footballers are nearly always unsuspecting. My own career with Mayo came to a halt well before my 30th birthday. I was conscious, as I called a long list of players at the end of 2016 to give them some bad news, that most careers are temporary.

There are no promises that a career will carry on indefinitely.

Two broken legs over a three years period finished me off, effectively.

First time, I was playing in a rugby match for my Command, which was really strange because I had never played senior rugby at all. I should not have been near a rugby pitch, not even in the same town, but I was walking across the square in Collins Barracks when I heard someone shout at me.

I had a bad head cold that week in November of 1987. Ballina Stephenites were due to meet Clann na Gael of Roscommon in the Connacht club final on the Sunday, and I was Ballina captain. I wanted to get something from the Doc for my cold. There was no earthly reason why I should have trotted out as a full-back for a game of rugby, but the shout I had heard had a message contained within and one that was no request. Powers-that-be wanted me lining out against Curragh Command and getting a result for Eastern Command.

Why that really mattered to someone on high, I have no idea, but three hours later I had broken my right leg, both tibia and fibula were gone in a late tackle. Doc Cahill, an old army doctor who had long retired, was at the game and he gave me morphine and put a slab on my leg to keep it as stable as possible. On the Sunday when Ballina lost in the Connacht final, I was in the Blackrock Clinic in Dublin.

I was not back playing for Mayo until the league in early 1989. My second leg break, my left, was worse. My leg was in bits and it needed to be plated, and that was the injury that sent me on my way to an early inter-county retirement.

The second break was in May of 1990, nine months after we had lost to Cork in the All-Ireland final. I was just 28 years old. Galway had caught us in the first round in Connacht that same summer. It turned out to be my last game for Mayo. The Sunday after losing to Galway, the Mayo senior championship got underway. And Ballina were playing a biggie, against Castlebar. A ball broke. Henry Gavin, who had been Mayo captain in 1985, went for it fairly. And he reached the ball slightly ahead of me on a wet afternoon.

I slid in on top of him, travelling on my bum and moving a bit like a banana with my left leg high up in the air. My leg went instantly. I was 20 minutes on the field waiting for an ambulance. I was brought to Castlebar General, and then to Galway.

It was the evening of the World Cup final.

I was lying there on a trolley, and there was a penalty about to be taken. And the porter wanted to push me off to theatre or somewhere, and I had to tell him... 'Wait!'

I never played for Mayo or Ballina again, and after lining out for Ballymun Kickhams in Dublin for 12 months, I called a halt.

At least it was my own decision, and not another man's phone call rudely interrupting my life.

I WAS WRECKED after paring back our squad for the start of the league. It was a full day of phone calls, and at the end of it I went for a walk in the woods to try to clear my head.

One of the hardest talks I had was with Niall Daly, who actually phoned me. He gave us so many options and we could play him in the middle of the field or at Nos. 10 or 12, but he had no interest in being a substitute any longer. We needed Niall, and in 2018 Liam and Ger and myself made a decision to make a fresh start and reconsider, and talk once more with everyone who had ever been in with us. Thankfully, Niall came back in.

Neil Collins, of course, wished to restart his life and forge a career in fashion in New York and his chat was the opposite of most of the others, and when I met him in Molloy's in Roscommon town for a coffee he admitted he might regret his decision, and was apologetic for walking away from us, but explained that he had to go.

Cathal Cregg and I had a shorter discussion, as he basically told me that he didn't rate me and that there was no big decision to be made between studying for his doctorate and playing football for a team I managed. It was tough to hear, but I had to take it on the chin.

David Keenan, Donie Shine and Seanie Purcell, all of whom had got so much game time in 2016, were also gone. In total, nine different lads from the previous season either left the dressing-room or were told they were no longer required. None of this helped the team stride from 2016 into 2017.

Ian Kilbride was away with the Defence Forces. He was a huge loss, as he is a physical, hard-working footballer who loves training and always set the highest standards for himself. He has heart and drive, and he was miles ahead of most of the lads in the dressing-room when it came to understanding the absolute importance of maintaining a strength and conditioning programme.

I wanted Ian Kilbride home, and I wanted Cathal Compton back injury-free. He could do such a big job for us at midfield or full-forward, he knew how to mind the ball, and he knew how to kick his point, but he was so unlucky with injuries.

In addition to cutting back on the squad, three players had retired at the end of the 2016 season, Geoffrey Claffey, Niall Carty and Senan Kilbride.

Geoffrey's decision I could understand, as I could Niall's, but at the same time Niall Carty was a monumental loss to the Roscommon team. He had size and presence as the team's full-back and he was also Roscommon's natural captain, but he had never fully recovered after suffering a cruel knee injury in London a few years previously.

Carty was everything any manager could ask for; he was rock solid and a leader of men, and he was humble, and there was never any nonsense from him. I talked to Geoffrey and Niall, but Liam and I had a longer chat with Senan Kilbride. We did so twice.

SENAN KILBRIDE IS such a magnificently talented footballer, and I had a great relationship with him through our time with St Brigid's together and afterwards. Other Roscommon managers had not fancied him as much, which I always thought was madness. He had a genius of a touch. I felt sure that we could build a massive county career for him in his last two or three years with Roscommon. But he'd had enough.

He was disenchanted with large portions of his county career, and he told me he had not enjoyed 2016 very much either. The first time I sat down with him alone, and we had lunch. The second time, Liam and I met with him in St Aidan's GAA grounds in Ballyforan. Liam in the back of the car and me in the front, and for 40 minutes we tried to convince him.

He was not for moving.

THROUGH THE LEAGUE campaign I did not hold back in my judgment of any of our performances. I was advised that I was being hard, perhaps harsh at times. Perhaps I was, but we had decided at the start of the season that everything we did and said would be enclosed by absolute honesty.

I used the phrase 'not cutting the mustard' quite often and not necessarily in a good way on a number of occasions as we got beaten and bashed from one round of the league to the next. That was me being honest, but perhaps I could have chosen my words a little more carefully. The reversal in our form from the first-half of 2016 was staggering to some people who did not know exactly what we were doing or how we had decided to back-end our efforts through the whole season.

After losing our fifth league game, we were the only team in the whole country, from all four divisions, not to have even one point in the competition. Since losing to Mayo in the league in 2016, we had played 14 games, won three, drawn one, and lost 10. The three wins were over New York, Leitrim and Sligo. I was also informed by one newspaper that we had given up 4-89 in our five defeats and that the 89 points was the biggest concession of white flags of any team in the four divisions. London were second in that department, allowing their opponents in Division Four to shoot 77 points.

I knew I was taking risks.

I had changed so much, including our training nights, switching from Tuesday/Thursday/Saturday/Sunday to Tuesday/Friday/Sunday, but the lads liked this as it meant they did not have to travel back home from Dublin twice in the middle of the week and that Friday's training session would dovetail with their natural return to Roscommon for the weekend.

There were good reasons to remain positive. While we were taking it lightly enough in training in February and March, I was hearing that Galway were really pumping it out as they were desperate to get to hell out of Division Two and Kevin Walsh was not in the mood to leave anything to chance. That information helped calm me, as did the work of our new strength and conditioning coach, David Joyce.

David's backstory was that he set out as a young man to make it as a professional footballer with Birmingham City but two cruciate knee injuries forced him to rethink his future working life. So, while we were not going crazy out on the training field, all of the lads were working at far higher levels in the gym. The first four months of 2016 had been torturous. The first four months of 2017 were lighter but smarter.

We had a great championship draw, too. It was Leitrim, and then either Mayo or Galway in the Connacht final. One game could make us Connacht champions.

I just needed everyone around me to stay calm. And I needed the players to believe in what myself and the management team were doing, but losses piling high leaves everyone edgy, and that included me when I closed the front door of my house behind me.

IN THE QUIET of my office in my home I could piece the jigsaw of my first two seasons as Roscommon manager into one complete picture.

Everything was about the championship.

And, by the time we opened our 2017 championship campaign, we would have played 15 matches against Division One opposition in less than 18 months, and we also would have played in two Connacht finals. That was simple maths. Seventeen games against the very best teams in the country. Win or lose those games, and even get our asses handed to us in some of them, it did not matter all that much once we were learning and getting stronger.

I JUST NEEDED everyone, me included, to stay calm. But that was going to be too much to ask in a county like Roscommon which always struggled to remain patient, and has a distaste for sitting in the backseat for any length of time.

The clubs were getting noisy. Some of them, principally the clubs of players who were no longer required by the county team, were unhappier than others.

But the calmness came to a sudden, jolting halt after our third loss in the league, when we went to MacHale Park and got beaten 1-19 to 0-14.

It was replaced by a month of wall-to-wall questioning. And of the most serious and personal kind, after a former Roscommon manager questioned my birthright to be holding down the job in the first place.

Before that, we were pipped at the post by Donegal in Hyde Park by a single point, 0-16 to 2-9, in what was a solid and very encouraging performance. They were three points up with seven minutes left. Conor Devaney then scored a magnificent goal, but they got their winning point in injury-time, from Eoin McHugh. But, seconds before that, we had the absolute winning of the game when our wing back, Ronan Stack was clear on goal. I expected him to take his point and put us one up.

Ronan went for his goal. His shot was saved, and they swept it back down to the other end. Ronan explained in the dressing-room why he did not go for his point and, when he was finished, having explained himself rationally, I was totally at ease with his decision. Also, I did not know it at the time, but there was a perfect trade-off for that same decision.

'There was time for them to go down the field,' Ronan said, '... and I was guessing they'd get the last point of the game.'

Ronan Stack had a chance to win the game for us.

And he chose to take that chance, rather than a point that might leave the game level, most probably.

'I didn't panic.'

'I knew what I was doing…

'We needed to win!' he stated calmly.

He had the balls to go for it. And a few short months later, in the Connacht final, Brian Stack, his younger brother, scored the goal against Galway that signed, sealed and delivered that title for us.

I've no doubt that in the Stack household, which is a home infused by a stubborn Kerry spirit, that what had happened in the Hyde against Donegal had been talked through. I've no doubt about that, none whatsoever. And, in the Connacht final, when Brian Stack won the kickout and surged towards the Galway goal, he knew what he had to do.

Everyone in the ground watching him was thinking… *Will you kick it over the fucking bar!*

But Brian Stack kept running.

Kick your fucking point! When Brian reached the edge of the large square he let it off and the ball was in the back of the net.

For me, that was the perfect trade-off, courtesy of the Stack lads.

Plus, they had heard me, ad nauseam, telling them and everyone in the dressing-room to think goals, and go for goals. Not necessarily when we were level or a point up with a minute to go! But if we were three points up with 20 minutes to go and one our lads had a choice?

'Go for your goal!

'Go for it!' I told them, '… and let's really put it up to them!'

TWO WEEKS LATER, on a Saturday evening, there were nearly 12,000 people in MacHale Park. Mayo had eight points without a single reply from us before the break and, by the end, they had 12 different scorers. They were that good, or else we made them look that good. I would suggest the latter, as they also had 15 wides over the hour in addition to scoring 1-19. It's simple maths. They made 35 scoring chances for themselves.

We did not win one scoreable free the whole game.

And that was not down to the referee, Joe McQuillan from Cavan. I never saw Mayo defend as brilliantly. At the end of the game, I had no idea what was being said about me on *Shannonside Radio*. But it was not complimentary.

The former Roscommon goalkeeper, Gay Sheerin was in the broadcast booth for *Shannonside*. He'd also managed Roscommon when he retired. But he was clearly extremely unhappy after the game and he was in no mood to tread softly.

He questioned why there were Mayo men on the Roscommon sideline. He did not like the look of either Liam or myself, and he said it was 'wrong'.

He also said he was laying the blame 'at Kevin McStay's door'.

This blame, seemingly, was for all of the players who were absent from our dressing-room. Gay Sheerin said our dressing-room had been split. He said that half of the room didn't want me. He said I had no county experience. He suggested that if Fergal O'Donnell was managing the team that every single last man who was absent might be back in our dressing-room.

'When you look down on the sideline,' he told his listeners, 'and you don't see a Roscommon person there... if there was a Roscommon person there's a lot of those players wouldn't have walked.'

He had an awful lot more to say.

And, by the end of the week, I heard practically every single word that he said. It was impossible not to. It was in the national newspapers every day. It was all over the local newspapers. It was on radio and TV, and when we played Kerry at home a week later Marty Morrissey questioned me about the whole furore live on RTE's *Six One News*.

All hell broke loose that week.

Quickly enough, I demanded an apology from *Shannonside*, on my own behalf, but also on behalf of my team and my management team.

A hellish week extended itself into a whole month of absolute nonsense. *Shannonside* refused an apology, and I pulled all co-operation with them. The players backed me and Liam and Ger.

I knew that I could never become a Roscommon man, but I had lived in the county for 30 years. My daughters were born and reared as Roscommon girls. My wife and daughters were upset for me.

I was angry that they were so upset.

I felt that on the street people who might never have looked twice at me, were staring. I knew people were talking *about me*, and not talking about me and the team and our performances. That was wrong. And I kept reminding myself of my father's advice to me when I first moved to Roscommon. He told me to make the new town my 'home'.

That was his word.

When he moved from Tuam and decided to live in Ballina, he also had made the decision to make Ballina a 'home' for him and his family, forever. There was no going back in my father's head. Neither was there any doubts in mine. Roscommon was my home, same as it was home for everyone else living in the county.

Neighbours, people with only half an interest in football some of them, were asking, 'What's all this about?'

'What did he do?'

I had support, too.

My family, my loyal friends. I had my wife's calm, clear-headed advice almost daily. 'If you feel you can make this right… and you are not going to make more trouble for yourself, if you are not going to bring yourself down,' she told me, '… then keep going!'

But she did warn me of the consequences.

'If this is going to break you,' she warned, '… or hurt you, or make you act in a horrible way to other people, then you need to get out of it… now!'

There was never any question of me resigning. I was too angry. And Verona knew how angry I was feeling and that is why she warned me about my own thoughts and actions. Other people had my back, too, and I could not have asked anything more of the county board. Seamus Sweeney remained calm and strong. We both knew that the natives were restless. Some clubs were now desperately unhappy. Quiet clubs had been fired up by Sheerin's comments and were asking pointed questions, but Seamus settled them all down. He told them that everyone would have a chance to do all the talking they wanted to do at the end of the season.

The thought of being fired did not sit well with me. It was on my mind all through the month. It was a matter of pride, of course, but my fear was also rooted in the person I am, and I have never liked things wrestled away from my grasp. Seamus Sweeney assured me I would have no worries of that happening on his watch as Roscommon chairman.

THE WHOLE DEBACLE had me second-guessing, everything.

My players?

Our supporters?

Myself and Liam and Ger, and everything we were doing? It was hard not to be in a state of doubt some days. We knew from the very beginning of the year what we were heading into. We knew it would be incredibly testing. All we wanted to do was to survive.

Survive, and learn.

And not be in smithereens when we came out the other end of the league, but close to the end it was getting to that tipping point. We were getting nothing out of some defeats.

Are they listening… do they believe me?

Are they trusting us?

The week after losing to Mayo, we had Kerry in town and we did okay, but Paul Geaney grabbed an injury-time goal to ease them to a 1-19 to 1-13 win. Ciaráin Murtagh had banged home a penalty in the 67th minute to reduce the gap to a single point.

We had been playing with 14 men for 10 minutes by then, and we were playing brave football. John McManus should never have been sent off on a straight red card. It was a ridiculous decision, but our lads responded. They really went toe-to-toe with Kerry.

Our fourth loss.

Our fifth was coming up on the rails, a 2-17 to 1-13 defeat by Monaghan! Our sixth, to Dublin, right behind that. During those two months, small things mattered and also other things, like the performances of Tadhg O'Rourke.

Tadhg had, and still has, no idea how he almost single-handedly allowed me to sleep some nights. Where do I start with Tadhg O'Rourke? Well, a great many people in Roscommon had not been huge supporters of his, and he had no real underage county career. He was from Tulsk, and he wanted to play for Roscommon. He gave me the impression that he was living and breathing in order to put on that amazing primrose jersey.

He was mad for it.

Throughout the season, we asked different lads, and also backroom people to stand up and serve us all in the team room a 'biography' of themselves.

It could be through Power Point, video, or just words. When Enda Smith did so, and talked about his brother's brave fight with cancer, it was raw and massively inspiring for us all. He was clapped by everyone for ages, and lads got up off their chairs and gave him a hug.

The biography was an act that revealed the real man to his teammates and the rest of us, and it was something that Ger Dowd borrowed from the All Blacks.

When Tadhg took his turn, he had photographs of Compton and Mullooly, his closest teammates, up in front of us quickly enough. He then took me on a tour of their friendship that I had known nothing about. He brought us all back to the United States, with the three of them. He introduced us to the three of them together in college.

We all understood what it meant to Tadhg to now be with the other two in the Roscommon senior dressing-room. I could see that the same dressing-room was Tadhg's big dream. And through his words, and his actions out on the field, in the league of 2017 I understood that Tadhg O'Rourke would die for his best friends, his teammates and the Roscommon jersey. When we won the Connacht title that summer, Enda Smith got the accolades and Enda deserved everything that came his way. My best player on the field?

That was Tadhg.

The narrative in the county was that he was not classy, not a stylist. The consensus was that there were better players who were not on the panel or lads who were in America. Lads who were constantly injured, and some lads who were not aerobically fit enough in my book. That's the thing with clubs and supporters. They do not have enough good information. Neither that, or true insight. Not enough of them had ever watched Tadhg O'Rourke at work four and five times each week for the good of Roscommon football.

I watched Tadhg's bravery in the middle of the field all through the league in 2017 as we got beaten, and beaten again, and he went for every ball. At times, cruelly, he left himself open. A more mature midfielder would not have stretched for as many balls as Tadhg decided he had to at least try to win. He got walloped at times. When I saw him get walloped, I looked at him and felt the blow as though he was my own son.

I'd stiffen up on the sideline as I awaited the bang.

LIFE'S MOST TESTING times also force us to smile, thankfully.

In the middle of the whole crazy, ridiculous, never-ending spring, myself and Liam went back to The Hatch for a late drink one Sunday night. As we entered the pub, Liam whisked off to the toilets.

But, immediately, I noticed that Gay Sheerin and some of his friends were seated directly in my line of sight. I skirted by them all, and took my seat at the end of the bar, and awaited Liam. I knew Liam was going to have to walk the same walk. And I knew Liam! I waited for him to say his big, friendly, all-encompassing 'Hello'.

He did not fail me.

'Howya lads!' said Liam, '… how's it going?'

He then sat down beside me.

'Liam… you know who you've just said hello to?'

He'd no idea.

'That's Gay Sheerin and his buddies!' I told him, '… congrats!'

IN TIME, I'D make my peace with Gay.

Nobody had died. And I was happy to put the whole sorry episode behind me. Though I did not make that peace until over a year later.

I was still too sore with him. He'd put me through the wringer, and then a lot of other people tried their best to keep me in there. That did not include Marty Morrissey, who was only doing his job when he told me he needed to talk to me live on the *Six One News*.

He was smelling a story that had me about to be fired.

Once Kerry had beaten us, and Marty had me out on the side of the pitch with his microphone pointed at me, the day had turned cold and dank. The hailstones had not started, not yet! They waited until Marty was half way through his expert questioning. Marty could see I was under pressure. He was viewing me at the bottom of the barrel. Four and zero after losing to Kerry, and Monaghan and Dublin to come.

I proceeded to almost drown during the interview when the rain came down. And then the hailstones started taking the head off me.

There was no umbrella within arm's reach. I knew, of course, how it works for RTE and understood that they had their two or three minutes to get their job done, until the satellite closes down, and that they had to simply keep going. Post-match interviews are always a pressure point for RTE and all TV stations.

However, I used one word during my interview with Marty, that I was happy to have presented to my detractors. I asked them did they want me to 'rebirth' myself?

When I got home shortly after, Verona wanted to know would I not like to tip up the town and grab a pint in The Hatch? I said I did not have the heart or the stomach. That Sunday evening was the lowest moment in my three years as Roscommon manager.

I was no longer sure where we were going. Neither did I know for sure who was with me, outside of my tight gathering of family and friends. I saw people looking at me, either sympathetically or with scorn. Of course I was imagining most of it. And hearing people say… 'Ah, the poor fella… no idea what he's doing!

'Why doesn't he get out of the mess?'

11

DUBLIN 2-29 ROSCOMMON 0-14
NFL DIVISION ONE (ROUND 6)
CROKE PARK
MARCH 25

JIM GAVIN BROUGHT his unbeaten run as Dublin manager to 35 games, and still wasn't at all happy with himself or his team.

I read his after-match comments the next day. In beating us, Dublin had finally expunged from the history books the efforts of the Kerry footballers from 1928 to 1933, who had gone 34 games without such a blemish, but Jim was sober as a judge, typically. He was polite to me, and decent, when we shook hands before and after. But when it was all over, he had also talked a lot of 'big talk' about the team regrouping and focusing on the next game and so on. His precise thoughts on defeating us by 21 points were hard for me to digest.

'We got a good performance here,' he told reporters, '… but we didn't get the complete one and that's what we're always striving for.' He went on in some detail, of course, but I sat there in my office in my house wondering just how thick was the outer surface of the bubble in which the Dublin manager sits and lives and watches games of football?

The evening before had been demoralising enough.

Gavin's thoughts were the kind that shovelled a whole lot more clay on top of the body of a dismissed opponent.

Dublin had only managed two goals in their first five games in their league defence, but they hit two more against us. Paul Flynn finished off a pass from Bernard Brogan after 15 minutes, and Kevin McManamon got their second on 57 minutes. In their 35 games without defeat they had, I read, scored a total of 48 goals and 556 points, or 29 points per game.

I was also forced to read some of my own post-match comments in the same newspapers, in which I used the word 'patience' liberally.

'People have to be patient with us,' I suggested. 'I know the patience is wearing thin at home. It's a young team… they're 22, 23 years of age. They're three, four, five years behind those big teams in terms of conditioning. And… people just have to hold their nerve, and stay with it.

'If they want to chop and change and get rid of half of them young fellas?

'And bring back what?

'It doesn't work like that!'

I HAD WORN the bainisteoir bib since the beginning of the year, and also I was no longer sitting high up in the stand at games. Unlike 2016, I was down at ground level. And in the trenches which extend from GAA ground to GAA ground.

Every time, it was a privilege to pull that bib over my head, even when I knew exactly what was coming next.

Like many of the greatest football and hurling managers, Jim Gavin gave me the impression that he was completely disconnected from what was going on in the world of his rival manager. A large part of me can understand that mind-set, which is usually self-centred and self-indulging. If I viewed any team I ever managed only four or five points up in a game, when they should have been nine or 10 points up, I could turn a little mental.

In the Connacht final a few months down the road in 2017, when we were beating Galway, I demanded more and more from our lads. We could not win that game by enough! With six or seven minutes left, Liam had to tell me to 'calm down'.

He took me by the shoulder.

'It's over!' he told me.

But my mind was foreseeing dramatic and drastic happenings. Galway scoring a late goal, and another. The game being snatched away from us.

'If he gives that ball away again… I'm taking him off!' I told Liam.

'He's coming… OFF!

'I don't care if it's the Connacht final!'

Liam was still looking at me.

'IT'S OVER… Kevin!' he told me once more, '… will you relax!'

WE HAD STOPPED at the Springfield Hotel in Leixlip on our way up to Croke Park for our game against Dublin. It felt like a long journey.

Knowing is the worst part. At team meetings before games like that, against a team like Dublin that is a cold, calculating, brilliant monster of a team, you know how it is going to end.

In the hotel, we talked. We revved things up, and we put extra shape on what we wanted to achieve that evening. But, at the same time, I understood that Dublin would not be having an off-night. They'd be ready. Every man would know his job in Gavin's dressing-room, right down to the tiniest spec of every position.

I asked the lads for pride.

I admitted to them that we were in a dark place as a team, but asked them to hang in together and hold together, tighter, tougher than ever before.

I knew we'd lose.

Everyone around me knew we'd lose.

The challenge was to keep it respectable. Six, 10, 12 points, something in that range! That might be deemed respectable by everyone watching. Plus, more importantly, far more vital, we might get to leave the field with our self-respect intact. I think we did. Maybe?

Croke Park is Croke Park, and everything that happens in the ground is accentuated and magnified because of the enormous size of the place. The game was live on TV. There were an awful lot of Roscommon eyes on us, I knew that for certain.

We lost by 21 points, but we never gave up.

We never bended the knee.

Or stopped playing.

IT IS THE easiest thing in the world for football teams outside of the tiny clutch of great teams in the country, to lose heart, and go through the motions, and do themselves a disservice.

Roscommon did not do that against Dublin.

However, it was only human to imagine myself going to-to-toe, and head-to-head, with someone like Jim Gavin with a more powerful team. With a team holding twice the ammunition Roscommon held in our dressing-room that evening.

If I was Mayo manager and I was taking on Gavin? That would be an entirely different contest, and to go into such a game knowing that I had every *right* to defeat his Dublin team and, indeed, that there was an *expectation* that perhaps I should defeat him and his amazing team?

In the depths, it is hard not to dream.

And that is no disrespect to Roscommon. They knew, as everyone knew, that once upon a time... twice upon a time, actually, I had wanted to be Mayo manager. Back in the mid-90s, and also right in the middle of Jim Gavin's reign as Dublin team boss. I might have been the Mayo manager trusted with stopping Dublin in their tracks in 2015 and 2016 and 2017, and planting that Mayo flag.

I had wanted that opportunity, of bringing a team up to Croke Park and entering that coliseum and, with everyone in the country watching I wanted to have a team going up against Dublin that was every bit as good as them.

A team, I felt, that I might be able to make better than Dublin on not just a Saturday evening in March, but on the afternoon of an All-Ireland final.

NINETEEN YEARS SEPARATED the two occasions when I rightly assumed that I would be the next Mayo manager. Nobody can argue down such an assumption on my part when I was the only man nominated for the job each time, first in 1995, and then in 2014.

Obviously, with two decades spanning this pair of disappointments, I had not spent my adult years either lusting after the job, or secretly conniving.

But I wanted it. Always.

Anthony Egan was manager back in '95 as Mayo's very poor league programme came to an end. The chairman was Fr. Noel Forde, and he had come to me to ask me to help out in preparing the team for the championship.

Maybe I was codding myself back then in thinking that I would be the next Mayo team boss, but I was of the understanding that the job would be mine by the end of the year. I had no say in the selection of the team, which was a crazy situation as I look back on it now. My remit was the physical preparation of the lads.

We beat Roscommon, and earned a place in the Connacht final against Galway. They gave us an awful trimming in Tuam but, as I did my time on the pitch as a water boy, or a future Maor Uisce, I got to view the past and peek into the future. There were four or five of our older lads on the field who had no right to be out there, but because of the chaos behind the scenes they'd managed to hold down their places. At the same time, Martin Carney's under-21s were coming through.

Within 12 months, Mayo should have won the All-Ireland because of the quality and ambition within this young group.

In September, I had gone on holidays to Boston with Verona and Emma, who was a toddler. On Pierce Avenue in Dorchester, I quietly planned my opening moves as the next Mayo manager. The job was still waiting for me back home. That's what I had been told. When I arrived back, I turned up at the next county board meeting, waiting to be 'unveiled'. The meeting was in The Welcome Inn. In my pocket I had a few notes prepared. The room was full enough, so I decided to sit somewhere in the middle, luckily.

Turned out, that was a good decision.

As the meeting opened and slowly got up to speed I sensed that there might not be a coronation. There was an edginess in the air.

The appointment of the new Mayo manager was arrived at, finally.

'Mr Chairman!' one delegate behind me piped up. 'I think we should put off this appointment for a few weeks!'

His motion was seconded.

And agreed in seconds.

I sought to get out of the room as fast, but as quietly as possible. I was mystified, but I was also annoyed, and deeply suspicious as to what had happened? And why I had been asked to show up?

'It's just as well, Kevin... that it didn't go to a vote tonight!'

*** **KEVIN McSTAY** CHAPTER 11 ***

One of my old friends from Ballina, John Kenny had caught me leaving the room and spoke to me in the carpark. 'There's been a sea-change,' he continued, '... and bar the Stephenites' votes, I don't know what else you would have got in there tonight!'

John told me that the other delegates 'fancied' John Maughan.

What!!!!

Driving home, all I could think about was John Maughan who... *Sure, he's one of my best mates!*

John?

We'd been in the army together. We'd driven up that road from UCG to Castlebar a thousand times together. We were minor together, and Sigerson. Played under-21 and won our All-Ireland together.

Why the fuck didn't he ring me... tell me what was happening?

At the same time, I realised... *How could he?*

He was in Cyprus, serving with the army in the UN. Nearing Roscommon town, I knew there might be a good chance that Verona would open the front door when she saw the lights of my car, excited to hear me tell her... *Meet the new Mayo manager!*

A couple of hours later, I was seated at the bottom of our bed.

What happened?

How did this happen?

I was close to tears, and I needed Verona to listen to me and try to counsel me for another couple of hours. It was close to three o'clock in the morning when I finally lay my head on my pillow and tried to sleep.

As I lay there, still not sleeping, I resolved to phone Fr. Forde first thing the following morning, and tell him I was withdrawing my name.

I hadn't looked for the job.

They canvassed me... why wasn't I told... if they thought I was too young?

I was 33, but John Maughan was a few months younger than me! His CV was bulkier. I understood that, of course I did. He'd brought Clare out of Munster and into an All-Ireland semi-final. *They think I'm not ready... that I'm not good enough.*

I knew I was not ready. Deep down, I did.

I'd won an intermediate title in Roscommon with St Faithleach's, and

I'd captained the Gaels in the town to a senior county title. But that was Roscommon club football. Maybe that wasn't good enough for some people in Mayo, I told myself. I'd also trained the Ballina basketball team to win the league and cup, but to GAA men, that was just basketball.

If they'd phoned… told me about John, I'd have said 'grand'.

Why didn't anyone tell me?

When John Maughan took up the position he finally called me. But it was a call to check to see if I was willing to come back into his dressing-room, and look to get back on the team? John wanted subs with experience in 1996 and, as it turned out, he could have done with some. I wasn't all that sore with John. I was disappointed, sure, but the reason I said no to him was that I did not think my legs were up to it.

Besides, I'd seen the young lads who were now coming through and earning their places on the Mayo team, and they were brilliant athletes. And they loved training. I felt old just looking at them, never mind running with them.

Would I have made a difference in the 1996 All-Ireland final and replay against Meath? I've often thought I might have, and the older I get the more I conclude that I probably would have, which is clear evidence of old age and delusion at work to form a very pleasant cocktail.

I never fell out with John Maughan. Though, at the same time, our old friendship has never been put back into one sturdy block of shared adventures.

We text.

At the right times, we wish each other well and tell one another… 'Well done!'

What was he thinking?

Why didn't he just ring me?

Those questions have remained in my head ever since, though I never presented them to John for answers.

JOHN MAUGHAN HAD a good, serious run as manager. Then Pat Holmes took over. And Pat was younger than me, too. He won a National league with Mayo in 2001, and soon after that my father was made President of the county board which was a role that made him so proud. I knew I still had my supporters in Mayo, too.

I'd beaten Billy Fitzpatrick to the under-21 job in the county in 1999, and did so against the odds. Was it a sympathy vote?

Did they want to show me a piece of their kindness, and at the same time see for themselves if I was any good at the management business? Perhaps. I'm not sure. I did my three years with the under-21s and almost won our All-Ireland. The Mayo senior job went back to John Maughan after Pat Holmes. In 2006 Mickey Moran was named manager, and in 2007 John O'Mahony took up the position again after a 16 years absence. In 2011, James Horan replaced him.

When Horan surprisingly resigned his position late in the summer of 2014 after such a magnificent tussle with Kerry, first in Croke Park, and then in the Gaelic Grounds in Limerick, I was greatly surprised. I was driving to Dublin from Limerick the evening of the game, with Liam McHale, and also a third passenger who had asked me for a lift as I came out of the ground.

Liam and I were chatting away about the game, when the man in the back seat, who'd been on his phone, spoke up.

'Well... that's you the next manager, now so!'

He'd just heard the news of James Horan's resignation. I was doing the evening edition of *The Sunday Game* the next day and I knew that Des Cahill would be thinking likewise, and would have to question me.

I did not want to give the wrong answer, or sound presumptuous, or even half-cocky about my chances. But I did not want to rule myself out, either. The job remained my life's ambition. Did I feel I was in a great position to win the job?

Absolutely.

'I'd imagine,' I replied to Des on air the next evening, '... that I might get a call.'

I'D NEVER WON a senior All-Ireland as a Mayo player, but the next best thing would be to win it as Mayo manager. I felt that with Liam and one or two others, that I could get the job done, and finish off the amazing job that James Horan had done. There were some great players there.

They were everything that we were not in the 1980s; real proper men, tearing into tackles, standing up and taking no shite from anybody. Mayo, even in Horan's absence, remained a football team at the very top of its game. Horan was responsible for that, and he was always prepared to do the hard yards and take the tough decisions, and take out anybody who was not in it for the right reasons.

He lowered the blade and out they went, and on he went with his team. I had a sense that I would have to do a little bit more of that. One or two of their biggest names, I still fancied could do something, but at the same time we did not score enough and there would have to be some changes. Also, Mayo did not respect possession, not sufficiently. There are so many good footballers on that team, who are all great athletes, and every time they give the ball away they expect to get it back just as quickly.

That was and remains a critical problem for the Mayo team.

When the date for nominations for the position of manager came and closed off, I was the only candidate. Ballina Stephenites had put my name in the hat.

The next morning, I immediately started getting my head around what I would have to do when I took up the position. *This is for real*, I told myself.

This has to be one hundred per cent flat out, from here!

A phone call from the chairman, Paddy McNicholas duly came my way, and it was agreed that we'd meet in Kiltimagh and start looking through my plans together. I was madly excited. The adrenalin was pumping every morning though, at the same time, I cautioned myself that some GAA folk, and certainly some of the older gents, might not be mad about me because of my *Sunday Game* work.

I had my head jammed with firm plans and general ideas. There was more on my computer. What I wanted to do and how I would go about doing it, and the support I would need in my backroom team, everything was worked out.

The budget I would need.

My plans for the players. My plans for the jersey. I felt that the jersey had been played around with for too long by smart designers, and Mayo needed to get back to a basic green and red. I wanted my Mayo team to make a statement and, remember, I was not going to meet up with the county board's main officers, the chairman, secretary and treasurer, for an interview. The job was mine. It was done, as far as I was concerned.

It was a long meeting, hitting almost three hours and for the first three-quarters everything seemed good and positive. We exchanged our thoughts. As a working meeting, it went perfectly well, and I phoned Liam on the way home and I told him that it had gone as well as it possibly could have gone, though there were a few bits that needed to be tidied up. They were not mad about the budget I placed in front of them.

'They think it's a bit too big,' I informed Liam, but quickly I also added that the Board knew the importance of having a backroom team that could give Mayo everything that our rivals, Kerry and Dublin and Tyrone, enjoyed as necessities.

The more I thought about it, however, the more I realised that the ending to the meeting was not good. The three men wanted to know what everything was going to cost? We actually took a break in the middle of this part of the meeting. When we all sat down again, they were even less happy with the figure I was estimating for the full backroom team and the body of work I wanted to get done with the team.

We met on a Thursday evening. I took a call the next day from the chairman. He told me he could not support me on my plans and budgets for the management team. I told him I would not be able to take up the job of Mayo manager without his support. I felt myself travelling back 17 years in time.

On Saturday morning, the chairman phoned me again. He had not changed his mind. I told him I would have to withdraw my name, so. I then rang Liam and told him where things had landed. Local radio had a story that I was 'out' and *Newstalk* was quick on their heels. The story was that myself and the county board could not agree terms.

Once it had gone public, I knew I was goosed. After an emergency meeting of the Board, I got another phone call. They had decided to conduct interviews for the position and they wanted me to attend with whoever else might have their names in the hat over the course of the weekend.

'I won't be there!'

I took my name out of the damned hat.

In the week that followed, Pat Holmes and Noel Connelly were presented as a double-act, joint managers. Holmes had publicly ruled himself out previously. But they got the job.

12

ROSCOMMON 2-15 GALWAY 0-12
CONNACHT SFC FINAL
SALTHILL
JULY 9

TIME TO BREATHE.

The past and our league campaign, thankfully, was an ancient story by early summer. The team was in the best shape of its life in my three years in charge. I never felt happier, or more confident about what we were going to do in the championship.

For starters, we were going to play football.

In the summer of 2016 we had not played the football I wanted Roscommon to play. We played the same kind of football that all of the bigger, stronger teams were playing, like Dublin and Tyrone, Kerry too. Donegal and Monaghan, Galway, they were all playing big defence, big turnover, and the sort of power-packed approach that was far, so far beyond us.

The one thing Roscommon matched all of these teams in was pure footballing ability. To beat any of these teams we needed to concentrate on that.

On our love and ability to play ball.

All of those great teams had given up on playing pure football, and I firmly believed that if we played our best football against any of these teams who were somewhat straitjacketed by their negative tactical playbooks, then, we had a chance against them.

Most other teams outside of the top six?

I expected we'd beat them most days.

AND, AT LEAST we did not get beaten in all seven games in Division One of the league. In our final game we had Cavan in Hyde Park and Mattie McGlennan's team needed points in order to avoid dropping down to Division Two with us. They had three points in the bag. I just wanted to win a game of football.

I didn't care who it was against.

I could not have cared less about Cavan. In the 37th minute they scored a goal that might have swung the game in their direction, but Cathal Compton slotted the ball to the net within 60 seconds. We won 1-13 to 1-10, but we really won by a bigger margin than that in my head.

We had two and a half months to savour that win because we were not due to meet Leitrim in the Connacht semi-final until the middle of June.

It was the sort of ridiculous and unreasonable schedule that characterises the GAA's prehistoric appetite for fixtures. But, I was not complaining this time around. It suited me just fine.

The lads went back to their clubs for a period, but we still had them back to us and had all the time in the world to top up on the work we had done in the spring. This was always our plan. It was this that kept us sane through the months of February and March, when too many teams were running rings around us or tearing up the middle of our defence.

I knew we'd have time to catch up on them. And, then go again!

For once, I felt I had numbers in our favour.

Up front I had the two Murtaghs. I had Conor Devaney. I had Mullooly and McManus. I had Cathal Compton and Seanie Mc, and Cian Connolly was coming good, and I knew he'd be even better with harder ground. Others too were hitting serious form. So, even though I knew that the countdown had already begun in Roscommon to the end of my tenure as manager, I was able to concentrate on the team forming in front of my eyes.

I was already marked down as a busted flush by many keen observers, who were awaiting either my firing or my resignation, after a short summer of football.

But I still found it easy to concentrate.

When we took Leitrim apart in the opening game of the championship, and finished up with a healthy 17 points difference at the end of 70 minutes, winning 2-23 to 1-9, there were still people watching us and telling us that we needed to think *defence!*

Some people were worried *for us!*

We were going to play Galway in the Connacht final. Galway had put 3-16 up on us in the final replay in 2016 and I was informed by more than one newspaper that although we were exciting to watch, our naiveté was going to land us on our backsides once again. I was told I was playing into Kevin Walsh's hands.

It was cited that Leitrim had scored 1-8 from play against us. And that if Leitrim could do that, what about Shane Walsh, Damien Comer, Michael Daly, Johnny Heaney, Tom Flynn and Gary Sice? And what about Gareth Bradshaw, Gary O'Donnell and Cathal Sweeney surging out of defence when they forced us into turnovers?

I had Niall Kilroy dropping back from No.11 against Leitrim, and sweeping effectively. I had him nailed down in that role in my head. He was in incredible shape, and therefore was perpetual motion, falling back, tidying and using the ball really well. But I was told I needed to do more. Man the barricades. I was reminded in another newspaper that we'd conceded an average of 1-18 in the league.

I was reminded of the ways of Jim McGuinness.

I was told that Kilroy had only one interception against Leitrim in defence, and that 12 of his 17 possessions in the game were in the half-forward line.

Our supporters and our county board read and heard all of this too, but, honestly, that did not worry me. Maybe Galway would cut us to pieces with their counter-attacking.

But, maybe we'd shove the game down the throat of their tactical plan first.

I thought we would.

I told our lads what we would shoot the lights out on Galway. I told any journalist who asked me basically the same thing. It was up to people to choose to believe me or not.

THE HIGHLIGHT OF our championship preparation was the long weekend we spent together in Johnstown House. We opened our hearts to one another for the three days. In training exercises we were flying, and almost *faultless*. In a game behind closed doors against Meath, we actually hit faultless for a while.

During the league there had been one major flare-up in the team room. I really went after players, and named them, for not engaging in the gym work required of them.

I made a huge issue of it.

A handful of the lads backed me. It was an open forum and there was no hiding. Those identified had to speak up. They had a choice of apologising, or making big promises and sticking to them. When they all came back into camp before the championship, everyone was committed to their personal Strength and Conditioning programme.

It was the first time I felt that I had a totally unified team. In addition, the breather after the league had given Liam and Ger, and me too, a chance to reenergise. Each of us personally badly needed that time out.

Everything was coming together, at last, and then in Johnstown House the switch was flicked. We had our free-taking ticked off. We had our restarts ticked off. On the ball, nearly everyone was making the right decision.

I was fuelled.

And, I was reminding myself of something I heard Ger Loughnane utter to Marty Morrissey. Ger was Clare manager. It was half-time and Ger was coming off the field in the All-Ireland final. He didn't just answer Marty's question. He told Marty that, 'We are going to win the All-Ireland!'

Two things happen after a manager makes that proclamation.

His team loses, and nobody pays any attention to his daftness at half-time. Or, his team wins, and everyone talks about the stunning level of belief of the manager.

That weekend, I was a manager who gave the impression that he did not have an ounce of pressure on his shoulders. And that weekend is still there for everyone to see for themselves, as we bought into a documentary maker wishing to film a 'fly on the wall' project on behalf of AIB.

It was called *Behind The Gates*.

It went up on You Tube at the end of the championship.

We agreed to it because we knew that we looked bloody good. We also agreed to it because the county board received a fee of €5,000 towards our team costs.

TWENTY SEVEN PER cent of Galway's scores in their semi-final win over Mayo came via the direct route. There was only one point in it at the end. But Galway had been the dominant team. They set the agenda in their 0-15 to 1-11 win in Pearse Stadium. They were four points clear when the game hit the home straight. Three frees from Cillian O'Connor made it a tight finish. I liked what I saw in the game.

Mayo lost Keith Higgins nine minutes before half-time, but long before that Kevin Walsh had shown his strongest hand. With the big wind at their backs, they went after Mayo. Damien Comer kicked their first point after 12 seconds after Paul Conroy had won the throw-in cleanly. Walsh had his men press up high on the Mayo kickout straightaway.

That pressure resulted in a smart point from Gareth Bradshaw from the outside of the boot. That was after 60 seconds. Two minutes later, after Bradshaw was fouled, Seanie Armstrong kicked them three in front. Armstrong ended the game with six points, from three frees and three 45s. Comer only scored twice.

But Comer was at the centre of almost every Galway blitz. And it was Comer who was on the receiving end when Higgins got his red card.

At all the key moments in the game, Galway pressed up high.

We needed to outpunch them from the start. We also had the greatest respect for Comer but we knew that we had the perfect man for him. Niall McInerney was tailor-made for the game Damien Comer would bring, because Niall is just such an intelligent footballer. I watched him being coached by Liam and Ger, and he was like a sponge. In 2016 he had given an exhibition of defensive play against Dublin in Carrick-on-Shannon. He is strong and fair. There is not a bad bone in the young man's body.

He's a bit like Ger Cafferkey in Mayo, in that you'd actually like to see a little bit of badness in him. But that's wishful thinking. It's not there. Not even an inkling of meanness. Comer, too, for all his physicality on the ball is also an honest footballer who totally ignores the dark arts of the game.

Comer would also end up scoring two points against us in the final. His second came late on and in the dressing-room afterwards I could not resist teasing Niall. 'You let Comer have a nice easy point there at the end!' I informed him.

We won the game by nine points, but we all know defenders are extra greedy even at that stage in a game and take pride in keeping their opponent down to the minimum score. Niall especially! Liam and I got to know him so well when we were with St Brigid's. Liam actually told him to get some sort of gymnasium going in the shed in his back garden, and get lifting. Niall was very young and still that bit scrawny when we won the All-Ireland club in 2013. By 2017 he was a very different man.

'I wasn't going to get too close to him!' Niall replied to me.

'I could see... THAT!' I responded.

I was still kidding with him.

But, Niall wanted me to know. He wanted to make certain that I knew what he had been thinking. 'One thing I was not going to let happen... was to let him go by me!' he added, clearly wanting me to know for sure that he was not easing off in any way. 'I didn't want him setting up something.

'I didn't want him getting a goal.

'A point was okay!'

My message all week to the lads was that Galway had absolutely no idea what was coming down the tracks at them. I repeated it that morning. I said it loud and clear in our dressing-room, and I meant every word of it. Galway had not seen us at all in 2017. Nobody had! The only people believing me, when I told them, were my handful of closest friends and my own family. Even my Mayo family were fearing for me and Roscommon. I could sense it from them in every conversation.

Did my own lads believe me?

I told them we were going to score goals.

That we were going to shoot the lights out on Galway. They were nearly all young lads starting out on their senior careers, and I reckoned there was no good reason why they would disbelieve me when I told them they were going to be too fast, simply too good for anything in the Galway dressing-room.

In the first 15 minutes, we scored 1-5.

And we must have kicked six or seven foolish wides.

Against the wind in the opening 35 minutes Galway managed just three points. Against the same wind after the change we scored 1-8.

We pressed them from the very beginning, and when they kicked the ball long Enda Smith was totally intent on winning every single one of them. He went close to doing that, too. Between himself and Tadhg O'Rourke we were winning far more than our fair share.

Our first goal was the sweetest thing.

Shane Walsh had just kicked their first point from play. Colm Lavin got the ball back into play with a perfect kick out the left wing. Seconds later Diarmuid Murtagh sent a brilliantly weighted ball into Cian Connolly. His man had already been yellow carded and, suddenly, he was one-on-one with Cian. Cian had that little bit of extra room and he was able to move onto his left and deftly send the ball past Ruiri Lavelle. It wasn't as breathtaking as Brian Stack's in the second-half, or as timely, because Brian's goal was a huge statement that told Galway we were not opening the door for them. There would be no question of a comeback.

Cian Connolly's goal did a different job for us. It appeared to suck the air out of pretty much every single Galway player.

From the first minute, we set out to lay down the law. We had a man-to-man press on their every kick-out, and our lads were instructed to only leave their man if the ball landed into the hands of a Galway defender who did not have a good first touch. If it was with one of the better footballing defenders, then our lads were to stay with their men.

Down our end, Kevin Walsh did not have them aggressively targeting Colm Lavin's kicks at all, and that surprised me. I wasn't sure what he was playing at. Neither was I too bothered trying to figure it out, to be honest.

WE SET OUT to make a row out of every kick-out.

I wanted to see if Galway had a real hunger for winning the 50:50 ball, and I knew that in their heads they had to be quietly hoping that the game would be pretty much the same as the replayed final 12 months earlier. Finding themselves in a fierce battle, how would Galway react?

'They won't want it!' I'd told our lads before the game.

'They will not want to fight for that ball!'

We had McManus and Mullooly clattering into everything in the middle third. They were soon bullying the breakdowns.

I told Colm Lavin that I didn't want many short kick-outs. Short kicks would leave us having to move the ball slowly the longest length of the field. I told him to take long kicks. All of our lads were ready for them, and more than ready for the battle that would ensue when every single ball was broken down from those kicks.

We ended up getting more clean ball than I had ever expected from Enda and Tadgh in the middle. But, when the ball broke we still wanted it more, and although we were the more intense team we found ourselves getting the majority of the fifty-fifty calls from the referee, David Gough from Meath.

He was dead right to give them to us, but sometimes the more aggressive team can be penalised for no good reason by referees. Gough had a clear head and he could see what was happening around him. We just wanted the ball more.

'WHAT DO YOU think will happen when we stick the ball in their net?

'When we score two, three goals?

'How do you think Galway will react to that? Think they'll be shocked? Think we'll be able to hold our nerves when we score those goals?

'We're going to score those goals, but don't get tight after it.

'We can't go into our shells after that!

'Keep thinking goals…if you think there is another pass…

'THEN GIVE IT!

'He'll have an even better chance of putting it in the net!'

That was the picture of the game I had painted for our lads for several days. And, at half-time, as Liam and Ger and I chatted out on the field for a couple of minutes and slowly made our way towards our dressing-room, our only fear was those same shells.

We wanted to smash those shells in that room in the few minutes we had available to us at half-time.

'Don't come to me tomorrow… talking about what if!

'I've spent too much of my life in Mayo dressing-rooms hearing players come out with that shite… myself too!'

'I've no interest in what you might want to tell me tomorrow… or Tuesday.

'NONE!

'Either stand up now, and do it… finish it.

'Or keep away from me!

'Keep away from all of us!'

I ALSO TOLD them that I believed in them, and that if they had taken all of their chances in the first-half that the game would already be long over. I told them they had to kill the game in the next 10 minutes.

It did not quite work out like that.

We stepped back from them midway through the half and they poured through for five or six points. It was down to three. There was plenty of time left. The wind was as strong as it had been at the very start of the game, stronger perhaps. A typically stubborn, crazy Salthill wind. It was getting tight, and then something happened that rarely happens in such a game. The referee spotted one of our men getting his jersey pulled 50 yards off the ball.

David Gough saw it.

But, even when referees see something like that their instinct is to let the team with all of the momentum to keep belting down the tracks. Gough, however, stepped in front of the Galway train. He awarded us an easy free. The game was back to four.

We won by the full glorious nine. It was the biggest win in half a century, or something like that, but I was not one bit surprised. We were ravenous. We'd had nothing for month after month after month.

It was not just hunger, however.

We wanted the game against Galway, and we could see how we were going to do it, almost as clear as day. If only every game could be as crystal clear.

Of the three of us choosing the team, I was the most conservative by nature. Liam and Ger would always be saying, 'Let's go for it!' They brought me along with them. The ball is in, the lights are green… WE'RE GOING!

That was what we wanted everyone understanding.

We told the lads not to worry about mistakes.

Mistakes were our problem. It was my job to fix mistakes.

Go, go… go! Go for everything that moves.

We weren't looking for mayhem! We knew what we were *looking for*, and that was all of the lads filling boxes! I'd asked Mick Byrne, a local Garda sergeant who was also our team statistician, to have his numbers on all of our lads with me by lunchtime every Wednesday. Mick had them to me by noon, on Mondays.

The stats on every player were there. The GPS reading, and every single little thing he did on and off the ball.

'Fill the boxes!'

That's what we had been telling the lads since the beginning of the year.

And at the start of the season myself, and Liam and Ger, would keep the boxes on the stats sheets to ourselves, but as the league ended and the summer came into view we began to send the sheets to every player individually. By the start of the championship we had all of the information in a group DropBox. Everyone had access to everyone else's performances.

Blocks.

Passes.

Assists.

Catches.

Turnovers

Steals.

There were more boxes, but those six were the six principal boxes. 'Fill all of the boxes!' I asked them all. 'And when you're finished filling them,' I warned everyone, '… we're going to have six men coming into the game who are also going to have boxes to fill.'

For me, the most important set of boxes of all on a Monday morning belonged to the last man we sent onto that field.

13

ROSCOMMON 2-9 MAYO 1-12
ALL-IRELAND SFC QUARTER-FINAL
CROKE PARK
JULY 30

THE MORNING AFTER winning the Connacht title we were all back in the Abbey Hotel in the centre of Roscommon town. We'd agreed to meet up at 11.0 and, for me, it was one sure way of calling a stop to one long night's drinking and to make sure that it did not lead directly into a second night of drinking. All of the lads had taken the Monday off work.

I'd warned of a roll call.

I was with my wife and girls throughout the previous evening, but such was the whiff of delirious excitement in the air that even I had struggled to get into my bed before 4.0 am. It had been one of the greatest nights of my football life.

'Jaysus… will you look at that…

'UP THERE!'

Someone had alerted us, as we came towards the town.

It was thronged. We'd got out of Galway by 8.0 the previous night. It was getting close to midnight by the time we were back home, but they had waited. Our supporters waited up for us.

At the team meeting in the Abbey Hotel I'd rolled out the plans for the following few weeks. We were one of the top eight teams in the country. We were heading to Croke Park. One of the last few gladiators still standing in the greatest coliseum. I'd always promised the lads, from the very beginning, that we would celebrate our wins, just as we would stick together tightly in harder times.

'When we finish an evening of celebration,' I'd also told them, 'that means the evening is over!'

They understood.

They had an entirely different mentality to the footballers I had played with in my days. The following evening we had a recovery session awaiting them. Time in the swimming pool. Some stretching. A sign-off on the entire weekend.

After we'd left the Abbey Hotel, we walked behind our captain, Ciaráin Murtagh and his brother, Diarmuid as they brought the Nestor Cup through the town, and led the team to one final pub for one final celebration drink.

Three weeks later we had a date with Mayo. It would be the first time that two Connacht teams would meet one another in a championship game of football in Croke Park.

THE OPPORTUNITY FOR Liam McHale and myself was huge.

We wanted to make our own county bleed, that is true. The jersey that we had cherished as young boys, and had grown to love when we earned it as grown men, was the jersey in our sights. We knew we had a great chance. We knew our team was getting better with each passing week, and we also saw that Mayo were running into walls. They'd survived, but they had played four games in five weeks.

Psychologically, that was what we wanted our lads to firmly believe. One more wall would be too much for Mayo.

'We're young... they're finished!

'We have the legs... they're tired!

'The last thing they want is another game... against us!'

At some stage I told our lads that Mayo would say to themselves... *That's it! Enough!* And I told our lads that we had to be ready to seize upon that very moment.

WE DID NOT get to know that we would be playing Mayo until six days out from the game. We'd all watched Round Four of the qualifiers with intrigue, but days before I had told everyone around me to get ready for Mayo.

'It's going to be Mayo... we want it to be Mayo!'

I thought of it as fate.

Weird, but a happy circumstance meant we would end up playing Galway in three Connacht finals in my three years in charge, and we would still get to present ourselves in Croke Park for a showdown with Mayo.

I had a sense that Stephen Rochford would fall back and would not press high on our kick-outs. Tactically, I was sure that we were in good shape. There was no way they would risk pushing up, not after all they had endured in a long and exhausting journey to the quarter-finals. In addition, I knew that they would be confident of getting the ball back, soon enough. They have that massive self-belief. Mayo enjoyed turning over the other team, and winning that ball back.

For us, however, in addition to winning lots of ball from our kick-outs, it was just as important to win more ball in the middle. Despite our performance in the Connacht final I still understood that, physically, we were inferior to most of the other big teams in the middle third.

We just had to look at the Mayo stats to know what we were facing. Beginning with Aidan O'Shea. While O'Shea was on the field, Mayo had won 58 per cent of their own long kick-outs during the championship. O'Shea had made six of the team's 15 marks. He had stormed forward and scored five points and assisted in 14 other scores.

All of the newspapers were talking up the meeting of O'Shea and Enda Smith, in a proper old-fashioned meeting of two colossal midfield generals.

Stephen Rochford had other ideas.

And he sucker-punched me.

ROCHFORD WAS NOT in the least bit interested in letting O'Shea and Smith battle until one last man was standing.

He told Lee Keegan he was taking up Enda Smith.

I was completely gobsmacked.

Keegan is undoubtedly the greatest man-marker in the modern game, and the performances he has given against Dublin's Diarmuid Connolly repeatedly showcased the Westport defender as being the ultimate distraction. A destroyer.

Smith was Roscommon's poster boy. That was not a particular role we wished him to have, but he had come to represent the whole team.

Our preparation, we believed, had been close to perfection in the weeks counting down to the game, and as we focused on Mayo in the days before the game we were convinced that we had everything in place. Every match-up. Every twitch that the game might take. And then, I saw Keegan standing next to Enda Smith.

What the fuck!

It was Liam who spoke up on behalf of us all… 'That won't suit us!'

Everyone knows, from watching Mayo in the biggest games they have played in Croker over the years, that when they want to take someone out, totally neutralise an opponent, they send Lee Keegan out alone on that mission. Keegan will always do what has to be done for the good of his team.

Whether it is fair and legal, or not.

Even if it means sacrificing himself in the process. Personally, I cannot think of a worse fate for any footballer than running out onto Croke Park in front of the whole country and finding Keegan awaiting him. He's as brave as a lion, and as fit as they come. And, as I've said, he is selfless.

As a footballer in his own right, Enda Smith is the equal of anyone in the country. He is two-footed, and he is so intelligent on the ball. He is a brilliant fielder, and when making incisive runs through the opposing defence he is clinical and damaging. After we drew the game with Mayo, we all sat down after training in Hyde Park and looked at some of the footage from the game. Near the end, we could all see Enda looking to run in one direction, but Keegan walked right into him.

Keegan tossed Enda to one side, sending him in the opposite direction. Keegan was the aggressor. Enda accepted his fate, and Liam found himself speaking up, asking Enda, 'What were you doing Enda?'

Liam spoke up for the entire group watching.

'You cannot let him dictate to you like that, Enda!

'You can't let him decide where you are going to run… you have to fuck him out of... YOUR WAY!'

We'd tried three or four times during the game to split Enda and Keegan. We moved Enda to No.11 and into the full-forward line, but everywhere Enda ended up, there was Keegan beside him, leaning into him, having the occasional word, breathing down Enda's neck.

It was a great match-up by Mayo.

Rochford knew Keegan has one of the biggest tanks in Gaelic football, and he knew that Enda has a smaller tank. By making that move they had immediately proven themselves to be superior to us on the sideline, too. They made us feel like pups. It was our first quarter-final since 2001. Mayo, on the other hand, have been having quarter-finals for breakfast for years.

The first thing a manager does in the very first minute of the game is look at the match-ups and, better still, have men in the sky to immediately verify for him everything on the field he had hoped to see. *Are our fellas on the lads we want them on?*

That's the question in the manager's mind.

He wants it answered positively.

I was standing there on the sideline, waiting.

Behind me, stood Ger Dowd.

In the stand, feeding Ger everything he was seeing from a great height was Sean Finnegan. We'd understood that Boyle, Vaughan, Keegan and Durcan, their massively explosive half-back line, would be in place, ready and eager to overrun our first lines of defence. That, we understood, would be Stephen Rochford's starting point.

And the half-back line is so vitally important in the modern game. When I took over in Roscommon, the very first thing I wanted to get absolutely right was our half-back line. It's the most critical line in football.

I wanted three very good footballers

I wanted them to be six feet tall, or damned close to it.

I wanted big engines in them.

That was the spec. Mayo had the best half-back line in Ireland and, in all fairness, why would we have ever imagined that they would break up that line and send Lee Keegan into the middle of the field?

Rochford went for our solar plexus, both on the field, and also on the sideline. The punch landed, too. It hit us hard.

Enda Smith finished the quarter-final with a single point.

Keegan, at the end of his afternoon, had one goal and three points.

'WE ARE HERE.

'And we are here on merit. We're Connacht champions. We hammered Galway, and there are no questions hanging over us.

'We have no apologies to make… we are the best.

'The very best team in Connacht.'

That was the message I had pummelled into the heads of the lads all week long as we counted down the days to the Saturday. When we took our seats in the stadium and passed the early minutes before heading to our dressing-room and preparing, our standing as Connacht champions was further enforced by watching Galway playing against Kerry in the first of the afternoon's quarter-finals.

Galway, and Kerry, were the curtain-raiser.

We're the main event here!

I didn't watch much of the game. Mostly I was concentrating on Kevin Walsh and his management team, and it smacked me on the forehead one more time! *Once the game is on, what is a manager?*

He's a spectator… like everyone else.

Whether you are Kevin Walsh, or Mickey Harte or Jim Gavin… it's overstated what a manager can do during a game.

Anyone saying otherwise… they're talking nonsense.

You can make a change, a substitution… you can try something, hope something different works.

Usually, it doesn't make a blind bit of difference!

Sure, Gavin threw in Cormac Costello in the All-Ireland final, when Dublin ended up playing Mayo at the very end of 2017. And Costello scored three points in a game Dublin won by a single point.

But did Gavin know?

He might have known Costello was flying in training. He might have hoped Costello's terrific speed could count against a tiring Mayo defence. Sure! This type of thing can happen, definitely. But, at the same time, if

Costello was not good enough to start the game, did Jim Gavin actually think that he would make all the difference between winning and losing the All-Ireland?

Gavin got lucky.

Simple.

AFTER 12 MINUTES, it was 2-2 to 0-1.

To us. Lee Keegan or no Lee Keegan.

What happened after that was accurately summed up in one sentence in the match report in *The Irish Times*. "The problem for Roscommon is that after scoring those two brilliant goals in the first 12 minutes," wrote Ian O'Riordan, "… they then walked off stage at the sheer fright of it."

No arguments with that from us!

It was 35 minutes in before we got another score after that start.

AIDAN O'SHEA WENT to No.11.

And we put Sean Mullooly on him, which was a match-up that suited us. Sean is a bull of a footballer, and fearless. He also has outrageous pace.

I was delighted to see them paired off.

'Go, go… GO!' That was what we had asked of Sean Mullooly, and that is what he did from the very start of the game. O'Shea's impressive stats were called to a halt by Sean. The best way to cope with a man like O'Shea is to run him. All of our lads had been warned about that. That was a big match-up for us and a huge success, and since we only ever did four or five match-ups in every game, it was a fantastic start.

Outside of those hand-picked match-ups, I was happy to let every other man just get on with his own game within our tactical plan. We had Seanie Mc sitting on Andy Moran, and he too looked fine. We had Conor Devaney on Kevin McLoughlin. We knew Conor had the speed to stay with him, and Conor did that the first day against Mayo. In the replay, McLoughlin caused havoc.

Niall McInerney took up Cillian O'Connor.

Again, an easy choice for us. We knew McManus, Mullooly and Devaney would bomb forward. Each is a fantastic athlete. Though Conor Devaney is slight and not a big tackler, and while Mullooly and McManus had strong running ability and size, they were largely inexperienced.

We needed our great start to calm everyone right down.

And we got it.

But we missed glorious chances once we went those seven points in front. Our first goal was a fluke, and if we had been able to pad out our lead with some of those easy chances we would have really sickened Mayo. Fintan Cregg was shooting for a point for our first goal but his lobbed kick found its way into the net. That was on nine minutes. Our second goal three minutes later was a work of art.

We sliced their defence open with a long kick in. Ciaráin Murtagh caught the ball, passed it off to Diarmuid, got it back, and struck the ball with total conviction.

I started screaming at Liam.

'Tighten them up… get in there, and tell them…!'

Liam did not even have time to leave our technical area. Within 36 seconds the ball was in the back of our net. Keegan was shooting for a goal and completely sliced his kick. It was a poorly executed shot. It was a poor decision, full stop from him. The ball was going yards wide before it was directed into the net off the back of Niall McInerney.

Teams are always most vulnerable after they score a goal. Everyone knows that. So, when you have scored two goals, and the supporters behind you in the Hogan Stand are going cuckoo, and you think you are suddenly in Disneyland, well, you are really in grave danger. That's why I started roaring at Liam.

I could see our lads were too high up the pitch. I could see lads out of position. They were not concentrating and the two or three tacklers that should have been in place to stop Keegan from going on a long run down the middle of the field in the first place, were nowhere to be seen.

It was the injection Mayo needed, and had been waiting for nearly all summer long. Not only did they cancel out our brilliant goal, they had scrubbed it out of everyone's head entirely.

WE CONCEDED ANOTHER six points without replay after Keegan's goal. Incredibly, they were two points up at half-time. Mayo kicked only four more points in the second-half, and shot nine wides. Our defence was quite brilliant despite the slippery conditions and the atrocious state of the pitch because the powers-that-be decided to open the gates of the stadium for a concert a week earlier.

We went toe-to-toe after that, but they were one point in front in the 73rd minute when Donie Smith hit a free from a million miles out.

I watched him line it up and could not help reminding myself of my words to him the previous summer after we'd drawn with Galway when he'd also saved our skin with a miraculous effort, but a shot that took enormous courage to make.

'You will never know pressure again… no matter what free-kick you ever take in the rest of your career!'

Those were my words to him. A big promise.

I hoped, as he weighed up his distance and steadied himself, that he also remembered those words. But he was so far out.

The ball stayed in the air for a long, long time. It stayed up there like an eight iron that Tiger Woods might have played to the heart of the green. Then Donie's ball descended, like Tiger's little white ball.

He made it.

Really, he made it fairly easily.

However, there was still time for us to win the game, and while Cillian O'Connor had three half-chances to tie it up for Mayo, we still should have won the game. We won the ball and had the greatest opportunity to one hundred per cent win the game.

14

MAYO 4-19 ROSCOMMON 0-9
ALL-IRELAND SFC QUARTER-FINAL REPLAY
CROKE PARK
AUGUST 7

SIX MINUTES OF added time was shown to everyone in the ground.

The drawn game was in the lap of the Gods. The game was into its seventh minute of added time when Keith Higgins passed to Kevin McLoughlin, but Niall Kilroy pounced. Niall made an excellent tackle. He robbed McLoughlin.

The ball broke to Sean Mullooly.

And Sean got his pass off, half a second before he was rugby tackled by Higgins. We had greater numbers in the counter-attack.

Higgins knew that.

I knew it. Everyone in the ground could see it, and we were sure to get one more chance for a point. Or maybe a goal, to slam dunk a famous victory.

But Higgins knew what he was doing.

He did enough to force Joe McQuillan, the referee to instinctively blow his whistle as he saw such a ridiculous looking foul right in front of his eyes.

It was 77.10 on the clock.

No whistle and we had Mayo beaten, and we were in the All-Ireland semi-final. Same as if there had been no whistle in the first game in the Connacht final in 2016 we had Galway beaten.

Each time, a referee doing the right thing by us snatched a famous win from our grasp.

WE HAD SO much to consider as we spent that week waiting for the replay. Starting with Enda Smith.

I was hard on Enda in my comments to the media after the drawn game. I accused him, amongst other things, of only 'pawing' at Lee Keegan. I probably should not have used that word, but it was the sort of word that I would have used if I was up in the RTE booth with Ger or Darragh.

It was one of those occasions when I realised I needed to edit myself more after games. Honesty was all well and good, but there are times when a manager needs to put his protective instincts first.

I knew that Enda had no doubts that I loved him as a footballer. And I was only making the comment for Enda's benefit but, still, I probably crossed a line. The problem was, we had spent so much time on the sideline talking about Enda and Keegan, and their duel, and trying to deal with a situation that was clearly to Mayo's advantage.

When we moved Enda into full-forward we had no sense that Keegan would follow him back. But he did. We had to get something more out of Enda. We needed to get him away from Keegan.

Yer man is wrecking his head!

I kept telling myself that, but Liam assured me that Keegan following Enda right back to his own full-back position wasn't the worst thing in the world. It was, in fact, the best possible result we could get from a tough situation.

'It's okay,' Liam said. 'At least he's back there... he's not going to score any more back there, marking Enda!'

Plus, if Enda was to fight it out with Keegan, that's where we wanted them to fight, right in front of the Mayo goal. Enda only needed one chance. A goal, or even a point, and he was right back in the game.

THOSE HANDFUL OF chances we had to add to our seven points advantage in the first-half were absolutely crucial. We had chances to leave Mayo crushed by half-time.

But we did not have the calmness, or the authority, which is a huge characteristic of the best teams, to do what needed to be done at that time. It was annoying, of course it was. And as a manager I had watched so much of our outstanding work essentially being poured down a drain.

Croke Park can make teams great, though it takes time. You grow as a team in Croke Park. The more you do the right thing, the more you win, the faster a team grows. After the drawn game I had spoken to the media about 'money in the bank'.

What I actually said was, 'That's money in the bank as we'd see it for the replay, and not only for the replay but for the next year, and beyond.'

I believed that, too.

But, even as I spoke about us being stronger and more confident for the replay, I fully understood at the same time that we had let a massive opportunity slip away. We just needed one or two of our men to be able to step up to the plate and kick those point chances that were thrown away after our two goals.

What happened?

Why did they snatch at their shots… shots that were…

Meat and drink to them?

Even as I tossed out those questions in my head, I already knew the answers. Thirty years earlier or thereabouts, I had been one of those forwards.

I had my chance to shoot a point that might have made all the difference in my career, and made all the difference for a whole county.

And… I snatched at it.

THE 1989 ALL-IRELAND final was ours for the taking for a crucial period in the second-half. We had Cork watching us, waiting.

I had lost a little bit of my pace after coming back from the first leg break. At the same time, the operation had been successful. John O'Mahony had been taking a personal interest in my training since the very start of the season. I was in Dublin most of the time, and I was missing some of the team sessions.

I was unsure what the future held for me.

But Johno was having none of it. If I missed a session, I'd get a call from him quickly enough and he'd say, 'I'll meet you in Castlebar… three o'clock tomorrow!' That was Johno's style. He'd be there bang on time, and he'd run me to hell and back. He worked hard on me, and as the year went on I got fitter and fitter.

I had a good game in the final on Niall Cahalane. I was ready for him. He was the enforcer in many respects in that Cork defence, the real leader for them at the back. Vocal, and always looking to drive the rest of the team on.

It was a game I could not see us losing. Cork had lost the two previous finals, in 1987 and '88 after a replay to Meath. In 1989 they had more than another All-Ireland final to lose. Everything was on the line, whole careers, and potentially a withering legacy of failing in three All-Ireland finals in-a-row. They led by two points at half-time, 0-10 to 0-8.

I didn't get off to a great start, and Cahalane beat me out to win a couple of early balls. Then I got going.

I only scored two points by the end, but I was making things happen and I was getting fouled every second time I got the ball. Michael Fitzmaurice finished the game with seven points from frees. Once the referee, Paddy Collins was giving me my frees I was not worried who was putting the ball over the bar.

Three minutes into the second-half Anthony Finnerty had scored our goal. That put us in front and three times the teams were level, before Fitzmaurice put us a point up in the 20th minute. Then Finnerty had another gilt-edged chance to score his second goal.

Everyone thought his shot hit the side-netting, but I actually saw the late John Kerins in the Cork goal get his hand to it. It should have been a '45' to us, and with the mood Fitzmaurice was in standing over the ball, I'm sure he would have banged it over. And we would have been two points in front.

We also hit the post twice and each time the ball came back into play, while Cork got two of their points from shots that went over after hitting the woodwork. The '45' we should have been awarded and those two unlucky rebounds were not the real reason why we lost the game, however.

We had three chances, after winning big possessions in the middle of the field, to stretch clear from them after Finnerty's goal. The second of those fell to me.

I should have been cooler on the ball.

Instead, 40 meters out, I snatched at my shot. I could have moved in closer. There was no good reason to hit it from so far out. Cork were nearing a panic at that stage of the game, and they were screaming at one another. I think I felt a surge of excitement, as the realisation struck me that we were primed to win the All-Ireland.

It was our first final in 38 years. The moment, when it arrived, to shut down the game caught us by surprise somewhat. It was early in the second-half, and the winning of it was suddenly in front of us. Those three chances were everything!

We didn't get many more of them, and we didn't score in the final 15 minutes of the game. Paul McGrath levelled it for Cork. Michael McCarthy, who like Kerins also sadly died far too young, scored the next two points. Teddy McCarthy then left them three clear of us. It finished 0-17 to 1-11.

Seventeen points, and only one of those Cork scores came from a free-kick. We'd talked round the clock in the weeks building up to the final not to foul them inside our half of the field. Larry Tompkins was the most lethal free taker in the country and we were completely tuned into not giving him any chances but, as a result, we probably gave the Cork forwards too much time and space on the ball.

I've never watched the full game since, but I've never stopped playing it in my head in idle moments. If I was a pundit for RTE back then I would have made such a huge deal of those three point opportunities. I would also have accused us of stepping back when the courage was summoned for the winning of the game.

We were confident of winning the game, as I've said, but it was a flaky confidence. I can look back and see that now, clear as day. The Mayo team I played on was riddled with that flakiness. Myself included, and if a goal went in against us at the wrong time in a game, most of the team would go into hiding.

We did not have the courage to stand and take what was ours, not when it was one hundred per cent demanded of us.

That lack of courage, and that flaky confidence, together they can make the best teams bend. I wondered about the lads in my care 30 years later.

They were tough, and mentally they were impressive, but I also knew that their confidence in themselves, in replays, and in big days in Croke Park, might quickly enough desert them. It was a genuine fear of mine.

And it was a fear I had to live with, because I could do nothing about it. The only way Roscommon could replace a flaky confidence with gold plated confidence was by remaining courageous, refusing to wilt under the greatest pressure, and winning.

The Roscommon team would have to walk the toughest of walks before they truly believed that they deserved to beat the biggest teams in the country on the biggest of days.

The replay against Mayo was that walk.

A TWENTY-TWO points defeat in the replay was not something I could ever have imagined. I did not see any variety of heavy defeat awaiting us.

Mayo were still low on energy. They were dragging themselves through the summer, and in the drawn game they had never shown the determination to rid themselves of us. Not even the slightest inclination. They were stuck in slugging it out through games, and it seemed to me that Stephen Rochford was unable to do anything about it.

I thought we had a decent chance of winning the game at the second attempt, but we would need to up our performance by a notch, and we would definitely need to be smarter than them on the sideline. I decided on two big changes in our selection. Mayo had so much power on their bench compared to us, and I thought it imperative that we should try to match them by having big impact substitutes.

I held back Fintan Cregg.

Also, I held in reserve our captain, Ciaráin Murtagh. We had assembled as a squad the evening before, in the Crowne Plaza Hotel in Santry, and announced the team selection. Ciaráin and Fintan were disappointed, of course. But we outlined our reasoning, and spoke of the massive impact the pair of them and our other substitutes would have the following day. By noon the next day I was getting text messages, which confirmed that our team changes had been leaked. It was so disappointing.

Only the lads with us in the room the evening before knew of the starting team, nobody else! Not a soul outside the closed door.

Both big decisions backfired on me and the team, and when Fintan finally went into the game he was chucked out of it just as fast and two yellow cards meant we only got 18 minutes from him on the field. By the time Ciaráin went in, we were no longer winning any decent ball and nothing went into him.

Neither of them had been hectic in the first game, but of course I wanted to prevent any sensational headlines announcing that we had dropped our captain. I've always hated that word... *dropped!* Ciaráin is a terrific fella, and Liam and Ger and I did not reach the decision easily, but by the Wednesday we had rationalised that we did not have sufficient impact coming from our bench. We wanted Caolfhionn Fitzmaurice and Cathal Compton to empty the tank in the first 35 minutes.

Then we'd have stronger reinforcements than we had all season. It was Fitzmaurice's first time to play for the county, so choosing him and excluding Fintan Cregg was a doubly big call. It was huge, but I was happy with him in training, and we needed a big man in the middle against Mayo. He ended up doing a good job for us.

I guess I had been hoping for a slice of luck to come our way as well. Mayo were entering game number eight of their season. We were a Roscommon team that had beaten Galway by nine points, and had shown ourselves to be Mayo's equal in the first game, Roscommon's first 'result' in Croke Park in 37 years, so I definitely thought we would play well enough to earn ourselves that little extra luck.

What I didn't know until the ball was thrown in was that they were without Lee Keegan. He was there, out on the field for the warm up, and he looked fine, but Rochford could not play him because of a foot infection.

I'd heard rumours.

That Keegan was seen in Castlebar General. Something about an infection. It was sensible to doubt all the babble, and distance our dressing-room from it, but as they warmed up I could not stop myself from taking regular glances down to the Hill end of the ground to see what Keegan was doing. He was fully togged.

He looked perfectly fine to me.

I'd made my mind up to start Enda Smith in the middle, and this time he was prepared for Keegan. He knew what he had to do.

I prided our group on being honest, and being straight talkers. Enda was in no doubt about what we thought of his efforts in the drawn game. I was sure he was ready second time around. Everything I'd said about Enda publicly was well intended. To his face, also, I had not spared him. I needed to be able to confirm that Enda had seen what we had seen, and that he understood. The most important act for every manager is to make sure that every player *understands* where he is at, and what he has to do next.

LEGS, LEGS... LEGS!

I left our lads in absolutely no doubt that we had the legs to finish the job against Mayo. We wanted to hit them early again, and have them hating the very thought of having to chase us for another 70 minutes. They were 13 points up at half-time.

They floored us. Before we even got going, they had us dumped in a bit of a heap. We were unprepared for them pressing high on our kick-outs from the very first minute. They were in our faces, and when we kicked long they were twice as aggressive in fighting for each and every breaking ball.

With no Keegan on the field, they had Donie Vaughan man-marking Enda Smith and seeking to do a similar job in harrying and hustling him. Enda did okay. But our match-ups, that had been exactly right for us in the drawn game, got us nowhere and Seanie Mc was soon being run ragged by Andy Moran. Ten minutes before half-time it was 0-6 to 0-2. It was okay, just! We hadn't settled into the game, however. They were laying down the law.

Then, our defensive structure imploded.

Kevin McLoughlin ran through the middle and planted the ball in the back of the net. Within a minute Keith Higgins gave Moran the opportunity to palm home their second. Four minutes later, Higgins carved his way through far too easily for their third goal. They would have had a fourth, but Colm Lavin made a point-blank save from Brendan Harrison.

All their defenders wanted in on the action, but particularly Colm Boyle and Higgins. They were breaking forward every minute, risking everything, winning the ball or coming off the shoulder of another man.

Stephen Rochford had looked at the drawn game. His response was simple enough, so simple and obvious that I had not seen it coming.

He came to the conclusion that his team was either going to die in its boots, or his team was going to die throwing everything they had at us. It worked perfectly. And their kick-out strategy was exactly right. We'd a good set of stats on our kicks in the drawn game, but that was because they had allowed us those stats. By deciding to push up high, they designated that the midfield would be the key battleground, and the only battle basically. There, they were bigger than us and more powerful, and hugely experienced. They knew well that such battles are won early, and fast. With their defenders ready, they were also going to have more men in that battle.

The story of the Mayo team, I guess, has been their ability to win more of these battles in the middle of the field than any other team and that includes Dublin and Tyrone, the whole lot of them. The Mayo players are simply brilliant at collapsing on the ball. And cheating.

I mean good, clever, legitimate cheating.

Knowing they have forced the other team to go long, every single one of their defenders take a step or two in front of his man. They are all ready to go. The half-forwards are also ready to race in. The midfielders know that if they break the ball, it's likely to be a Mayo feast. As soon as the ball is kicked, they've packed the area.

Every time, they had as many as six lads 'collapse' in on the breaking ball. It left us winning a broken ball in this area down to a matter of outrageous courage or luck, and probably both. Mayo hit that contact area with massive speed, too.

They wiped us off the face of the middle third of the field.

It took brilliant athleticism from them. It also took footballers who were prepared to take the high risk road. But with their athleticism and power and speed, that risk is essentially shrunken down to something that is not all that sizeable and not a big worry for Stephen Rochford.

They came at us in waves.

When we went short, they had so much pressure at work that the ball usually went over the sideline. Every time, they dared us to go short. They stood off, maybe six metres from their man, maybe slightly further back than that, but they knew that they could make up that same amount of ground while the ball was in flight.

They shut us down.

On the sideline, they shut us up. For those last 15 minutes of the first-half I could not even think.

2018

15

ROSCOMMON 4-16 CAVAN 4-12
NFL DIVISION TWO FINAL
CROKE PARK
APRIL 1

IN 2018 WE got back to our third Connacht final in-a-row. Galway again. We had only one step to take to the final and that was to step over Leitrim, again. We beat them by 14 points, and we were in our dressing-room in Carrick-on-Shannon and we were not even half as happy as we should have been after an all-round decent performance.

I saw an opportunity to even further unite our lads.

Make them believe that it was Roscommon against the world, if you like! I wanted to steel ourselves for what looked like a defining game, for everyone in the dressing-room, probably me included.

After three meetings with Galway in Connacht finals it stood at one win each, and one drawn game, so 2018 was a game that would ultimately decide who really were kings of the place.

In 2016, we'd played Galway in Salthill and the replay was brought to Castlebar, because our ground was not fit for the purpose. In 2017 we were back in Salthill. I knew that if we qualified for our third final the Connacht Council was thinking Salthill or Castlebar, once again. Hyde Park was not on the short list of possible venues for the final.

I did not wish to create a siege mentality within our group, not entirely. That can be a dangerous thing and sometimes such a strategy can collapse in upon a dressing-room. But I wanted our lads to believe that we were being disrespected, and that in the heads of the power brokers in Connacht only Mayo and Galway seriously mattered.

'Are we ever going to be allowed to play a Connacht final in our own field?'

That's the question I put to the room.

I then waited for answers, because I wanted a buy-in from every single man in the room. It was not something I wanted to lead. I wanted my management team to stand by our team, and for the whole lot of us to say... 'NO!'

I got back into the dressing-room fast after the final whistle. 'We have an important decision to make,' I began, '... and I want us to make it here and now!' Everyone was in the room. I'd asked for lads getting some treatment in the next room to stop what they were doing and join us. I had all the county board officers in with us. If we decided on shouting out 'NO' then I wanted it to be one loud Roscommon voice.

'There can be no rowing back from this, by anybody,' I warned them, looking around at all of the faces. 'If we say yes, then we say yes!

'And, if we say no, then we will all live by that no!'

I said I would agree with whatever decision the group reached. I told them that we had the power to unleash the ultimate sanction and tell the Connacht Council where the final was going to be played.

'It may end up that we do not get to play in the Connacht final... and, if that is the case, we'll live by that, too. But that is the worst-case scenario.' Everyone was in agreement that the only place the final was going to be played was Hyde Park.

'So...' I told everyone, finally, 'I'm going to go out that door and I am going to tell everyone waiting out there, all the journalists out there, that it is Hyde Park or nowhere as far as we are concerned.

'I'm going to tell them that we will not show up for a Connacht final in any other football ground... right?'

There were 'Yeses' on every side of me, and before anyone could open their mouth and say another word, I left the room.

A FEW WEEKS LATER I received a phone call from Cian O'Neill, the Kildare manager, who wanted to ask for some advice. He had been told by the men in Croke Park who decide on fixtures that their qualifier game against Mayo could not be played in St Conleth's Park in Newbridge, Kildare's home field.

O'Neill wanted to know how we had managed it in Roscommon, how we had stood up to the Connacht Council and stood our ground, and won.

From that conversation, he soon ended up on the *SIX ONE NEWS* on RTE telling the whole country, but in particular the gentlemen in Croker, that they would be turning up in their own ground to play Mayo and that they would not be turning up anywhere else in the country.

'Newbridge or Nowhere' was born.

AS ROSCOMMON MANAGER, I felt it was my duty to stand up and demand that the Connacht final be played in our home ground.

I could not have stood up in front of my own players if I had allowed the game to be played elsewhere. In fairness, everyone was shoulder-to-shoulder with me, including the brave county board officers. Of course, I had also correctly sensed that the media would love our cause. The majority of journalists fight for players when they take on the bureaucrats sitting around tables.

Our chairman, Seamus Sweeney and I chatted. We agreed I would do the television interviews, he would do the radio interviews. The final will be in Hyde Park and we are not meeting with anyone to talk about any other ground or any compromise. That was the simple message.

Typically, the Connacht Council took their time getting back to us. They let us stew for a week or so. I knew that that made our Board a little uneasy, because they had to deal with the officials in the Council on a weekly and monthly basis on all sorts of issues, including Roscommon's perilous financial position. For me, there was also a personal issue as the secretary of the Connacht Council, John Prenty has been a friend of mine through most of my adult life.

I felt really bad doing that to John.

My belief, genuinely, is that players should play, managers should manage, and administrators should administer. That is how the GAA world should work, all of the time. So I was stepping out of line with my own basic beliefs.

Also, the truth of it is, the Roscommon Board had allowed Hyde Park to reach such an awful state that it was nearly impossible for the place to host a big match, and it definitely was in no fit state for the 2018 Connacht final. I knew it would take a massive effort in a very short period of time to try and get it even half-right. That effort was forthcoming, immediately. When I had a look around the place in the weeks that followed, and I did so nearly every day, I saw many of my players' fathers and mothers cleaning seats in the stand, and painting the place, trimming, tidying up anything that could be tidied.

That made me extra proud, but it should never have a reached a point where the parents of a Roscommon footballer would have to wash bird shit off seats.

But the people of the county, generally, were delighted that we had stood up for ourselves and also for them. The game being played in the Hyde was also going to mean a very important uplift to businesses in Roscommon town for the day. On the Thursday before the game, I still felt that I was guilty of damaging my friendship with John Prenty, however. I needed to reach out to him.

I had to do what I did.

If I had not spoken up then the Board would have just rolled over and allowed the final to be played in Salthill or Castlebar. And the players would have knuckled down and kept their mouths closed. So, two days before the final I wrote a long letter to John Prenty. I made sure that he did not receive the letter until the Monday or Tuesday morning.

"You have done some good and amazing things for me in my life," I admitted in the letter. "All I can ask of you now is to see what I have done, and understand that in my role as Roscommon manager I had to do this.

"Whatever happens on Sunday, we will always be friends, I hope."

I told him it was not personal

It was only GAA business.

As I stood on the sideline on the Sunday, just before the National anthem was played, I saw John a few yards off, standing next to the Nestor Cup. He looked back at me, and I walked up to him and gave him a hug.

He reciprocated.

'We will always be friends!' I told him.

'We will!' he told me. And I told him I had a note in the post.

Then!

My head finally one hundred per cent clear, it was game on! Me and Kevin Walsh... Roscommon and Galway, in one final game to decide who were the rightful champions of Connacht.

FIVE YEARS EARLIER, I had proven myself one of the very best managers in the club game. I did so with the considerable help of Liam McHale and Brendan 'Benny' O'Brien and the finest of support from the people in St Brigid's, but it's the way of things in the GAA that the man wearing the bainisteoir bib on him gets nearly all the plaudits. Or else, a dagger in his chest.

The manager is the man who wins. Or loses.

It's thanks to him, or it's his fault entirely. Which is entirely wrong, of course, and in my three years managing Roscommon I got to weigh up from close range the worth of the men who were allegedly the smartest of the smart on the county stage.

Jim Gavin.

Mickey Harte and Eamonn Fitzmaurice. And the likes of Rory Gallagher in Donegal. Kevin Walsh, too. I was competing against them with an inferior force, or a group of footballers who had not yet developed to their fullest potential. It left me feeling that little bit disadvantaged, just like Andy McEntee in Meath and Kieran McGeeney in Armagh have been fighting uphill.

The likes of us, working outside of the Big Three and without their processes and brilliant support systems, have to be performing to our very best every single day if we are to be successful. We can hardly afford even one down day.

We have to be brilliant or miraculous or downright lucky, and of course that is not likely on a consistent basis. It was different when I was with St Brigid's and we went after the All-Ireland title. I was managing a team of seasoned, vastly experienced footballers who had already achieved almost everything, and had made it clear in All-Ireland club finals and semi-finals that they were amongst the best of the best. It was my job to find another one or two per cent within that group and help them win that elusive All-Ireland title. I had hoped to do exactly that with Mayo in 2015.

It was a whole different job to my job as Roscommon manager. The two were bodies of work on entirely different planets.

When St Brigid's qualified for the All-Ireland club semi-finals in 2013 we were in the company of Crossmaglen Rangers, Ballymun Kickhams and Dr Crokes from Kerry. And I was in a contest with John McEntee, Paul Curran and Pat O'Shea, up against three of the very best club managers. I felt their equal. If I was a fighter, then I was in my corner listening to the legendary ring announcer, Michael Buffer shout it out... 'LET'S GET READY... TO... RUMBLE!!!!'

If I was in that corner, touching my gloves, I would have had a confident smile on my face, too.

We met Crossmaglen Rangers in our semi-final, and when it was all over I went into the opposing dressing-room to commiserate and as I was speaking I could see John McEntee sitting down to my right. His head was in his hands. Rangers had been beaten by the slimmest margin possible, but he looked to me like a man who had taken the beating of his life and, as I continued to speak, I fully understood what it all means to a man like McEntee.

He had not come into our room. It had been explained to me that it was not an act of disrespect. The man was simply distraught, I was told. I accepted that. Crossmaglen were wired to win another All-Ireland title. It was what they did, and it was what they expected of themselves.

Everything they had won! And, still, losing in 2013 was like the end of the world to McEntee!

We had played them in Mullingar. We knew how they would look at us, that they would see us as a team from the west, and a team that could be pushed back into its box. And a team that, ultimately, would accept being pushed back, boxed away, and take its place on the shelf with all of the other teams deemed not quite good enough to win the 2013 All-Ireland club title.

We knew they would be hard.

They would bring a tough, intimidating game, stretching fairness right to its limits. We knew they would not be nasty. Crossmaglen Rangers are too good a football team to bother themselves with very much of that.

'Not today!'

That was the message I placed in the heads of our lads. There would be no stepping back. Nobody was going to push us around, either. Benny O'Brien, one of the club's great men and an assistant coach with me, worked so hard on drilling home that message in the dressing-room.

Sean Kilbride, another great Brigid's man had promised me something when I accepted the job. 'I'll tell you one thing they will do for you, Kevin,' he stated. 'They'll keep playing for you... they'll never stop! No matter what they're hit with!'

That stubborn spirit was alive and thriving in the DNA of the team. I found that out fast enough earlier in the season, but the mental game against a team like Crossmaglen was practically *everything*. To win the Connacht title we'd had to go to Galway and Mayo, and beat the two best clubs in each county away from home. We beat Ballaghdereen easily enough. Before the game I'd told the lads... 'If we think we can win this game by 10 points, then let's go out there and win it by 10 points.

'Why should we only win it by two or three points?'

That was the message myself and Liam left with the lads all of the time. If we thought we could stuff a team, then go and stuff them.

They were a confident, mature bunch in the room. I knew I could tell them how good they were and how much better they were to every other team. And I knew that it would not go to the head of even one player. Instead, that total belief would settle contentedly into every head. When we went to Salthill, who had absolutely murdered Brigid's only a few years before, I told them... 'We should beat these by... six or seven points, at least! If we don't... anything less than that, and we're not going to do ourselves justice.'

Our preparation, of course, had to be meticulous in order to totally back-up the promise of such big victories. And it was, and as a result St Brigid's was a team with gold standard confidence.

It was the real thing.

IT WAS HARDLY ever like that while I was with Roscommon.

Apart from the evening before the 2017 Connacht final when we all met up in the Abbey Hotel and I told the lads... 'Isn't this unreal!'

'We are here, and we are soon going to go to bed and we are totally focused. And there are 30 footballers going to bed in Galway tonight and they have no idea what is ahead of them tomorrow.

'They haven't a clue!'

I promised all the lads around me and Liam and Ger, that if we played, really played as we could play, then we were going to wipe Galway off their feet. I knew we had scoring forwards, and I knew they were completely primed.

'Let's not leave anything to doubt… I want us to destroy them tomorrow.'

IN THE CAR, going to all of our St Brigid's games, the three of us had this little game we liked to play. Myself and Liam and Benny would tell one another exactly how much we were going to win by.

Liam's prediction was the boldest before we played Ballymun in the All-Ireland final. 'I think we'll take them by a clear five!' At half-time, as we walked off the field, he quietly admitted that Ballymun had surprised him. 'I never thought they were as good as this!'

All through the year we had worked at developing personal team messages that we would live and die by. They stared back at the whole lot of us in every room we entered, whether it was a hotel room for a meeting, or a dressing-room we were entering for the first time.

HONESTY OF EFFORT.

And.

ABSENCE OF EGO.

We also had a team goal that we set out to achieve at the beginning of the season. It was going to be tough, but we all decided to go for it. We wanted to play in one near perfect game where we'd score more in the second-half that we did in the first-half and, also, concede less in the second-half than we did in the first-half.

It might not sound so incredibly hard. But, believe me, a team playing to its fullest potential has to reach for a simply astonishing performance to do that. Say, for instance, you are seven or eight points up at half-time having scored 1-12. You have to go out in the second-half, for starters, and end up with 2-25. We only managed it once all season long, and that was in the All-Ireland final against Ballymun Kickhams when they threatened to sweep us off our feet and led by 2-3 to 0-1 after 10 minutes.

At half-time they led 2-6 to 1-5

We took the game, 2-11 to 2-10.

IT WAS QUITE amazing, in many respects, to work with a Roscommon club that had confidence of gold standard and who, even eight points down in Croke Park, never stopped believing in themselves and their right to win a game of football. Roscommon as a county was not within reach of the same self-worth when the biggest days arrived.

Playing for so long in Division Two and only getting to briefly sample for a couple of seasons what football in the higher division was like, did not help this situation. And we were back in Division Two for 2018. We managed to show that we were too good to be back down there and, despite a dodgy opening game with Meath in Hyde Park when we relied on a dubious penalty decision to earn a share of the points, we were able to win promotion with Cavan.

We got back up, without setting the world on fire.

Roscommon 2-12, Meath 2-12.

Tipperary 3-9, Roscommon 1-17.

Roscommon 0-7, Down 0-12.

Louth 0-12, Roscommon 1-21.

Clare 2-12, Roscommon 2-19.

Roscommon 0-15, Cavan 0-13.

Roscommon 0-17, Cork 1-11.

I was still conscious of how we handled the lads in the early months of the season, and what we demanded from them. Like many counties in the west and in the midlands, every training session listed in the diaries of the majority of our players was extra time consuming. We had 21 of our lads living in Dublin when our season kicked off in January. The Club Rossie bus was not practical for ferrying them all from different parts of the city, so we had three taxis in operation from different locations.

This, of course, added to the costs for the county board. Because I wanted to go lightly on the lads in February and March, and only have one midweek session, the burden was eased in the opening months. The other problem, however, was our training base.

We still didn't have one, not really and the Kiltoom club were generous to a fault in facilitating us. In 2017 we'd been in Kiltoom and Athlone Institute of Technology. In 2016 it was Kilbride. Without a true home for the team, I still felt we were at a disadvantage during those important early months when every team is settling in and setting out its stall for the year ahead.

I knew what we had to work on in the early months, too. We were scoring freely against Division Two teams, because we would always find one or two chinks in the opposing defensive armour, but at the same time we were giving away fairly big scores.

By the end of the campaign we were the highest scoring team in the country. The satisfaction in that, however, was neutralised by the fact that we were still not embracing the concept of hard tackling.

Getting out of Division Two was something I was promising the Board, and for everyone in the dressing-room it was a personal priority. That's why I expected a little bit more of the hard work and grind in our own half of the field. I wanted the whole team to buy into the massive lift that comes with a big block or a good hit on a man.

We had a few players who were eager to engage but, the team as a whole? Even in Division Two we were not putting the required heat on other teams. We swept well. We did a lot of tackling, I have to say. We just didn't do enough bossing or bullying, which should be expected from a team which felt that it was misplaced living and playing outside of Division One. Games were also more competitive than I had expected.

It was my first time in Division Two, and I wasn't sure what to expect. We were the firmest of favourites to bounce right back up to the top division, but after three games we had just three points and one of those we had not deserved. Andy McEntee, the Meath manager and his brother, Gerry, the hero from the county's All-Ireland wins in the 80s, were both so annoyed afterwards they could barely speak with me.

I just apologised. 'That's the way they go,' I told Andy. 'It could have been me feeling what you are feeling, just as easily!' When Meath got a late penalty against Kildare 12 months later and finally secured promotion back to Division One after so long, I texted Andy and typed just one word.

"Karma!"

Our five points defeat by Down, in front of our own supporters, was close to being an absolutely horrendous performance all round, from defenders and forwards, and also us as a management.

Against Tipperary in Semple Stadium, a week earlier, we had been six points behind far too close to the end of the game. We had to score a goal and five points without reply in the final eight minutes to escape with both points. They'd scored from the penalty spot in the first-half through Conor Sweeney. Another penalty from the same player in the second-half had them 2-8 to 0-7 in front, and we looked in bigger trouble. A Diarmuid Murtagh goal two minutes from the very end got us level. Four minutes into stoppage time we went ahead when Conor Devaney popped the ball over. Donie Smith got our final point.

It was relieving, but it was no way for an allegedly big team from Division One to win a game in Thurles. Then, seven days later, we were down to 14 men midway through the first-half when Ian Kilbride was sent off against Down.

The defeat to Down was the poorest performance in my whole three years in charge of the team, and I did not hide my disappointment afterwards. I told reporters that maybe the Roscommon team and management were 'not good enough for Division One'. It was a comment that did not go down well with some people in the county, but I wanted the truth to hurt. Maybe we were simply not good enough, not yet.

We needed to win our last four games in the group to get back up. In the middle of February that looked a big ask.

OUR WINS OVER Louth, Clare and Cavan were bloody hard work. The two points win over Cavan in Hyde Park was earned after another big finish, as we hit five points in the last 15 minutes of the game, to their single effort. Ciaráin Murtagh hit three of those points for us, really late.

After we managed a three points win over Cork, we had another meeting with Cavan in the Division Two final in Croke Park. We were back in Division One and it was a game we could afford to lose and, at the same time, could not even *think* of losing.

The story of Roscommon football during my lifetime living in the county has been one of disappointment. That, and the always niggling question in the heads of players... *Is it going to be worth it?* We had only three players left in our squad who had been on the Roscommon team that brought home the All-Ireland minor title in 2006.

Think about it? In 2010, eight lads from that minor team were in the senior team that was managed by Fergal O'Donnell and triumphed in the Connacht final against Sligo. Conor Devaney was 22 years old that summer and he missed out on that win because he decided to spend his summer working and playing football in San Francisco. Conor was only doing what young men in Roscommon regularly decided, and came down on the side of a summer away. Conor, interestingly, was one of the three young boys from 2006 still with us in 2018.

Was 2018 going to be worth it?

I'd guess every single man who wears the Roscommon shirt thinks that to himself every single year. It's a question that players in the best counties, Dublin and Kerry, never countenance.

So, the smallish matter of a Division Two final against Cavan, in Croke Park, should be viewed against that backdrop. It was a chance to win a game we were expected to win. It was a chance to win silverware. Lastly, it was a chance to show the country, and our future opponents, that we weren't half bad.

At the end of the same game, I'd no real idea what people thought about us. I was in a bit of a dither myself, in all honesty. I was still convinced that our biggest weapon was going forward with the ball. Playing ball. If we decided to defend, and defend and defend, and put 12 men behind the ball at all times, I'm not sure what we would have achieved. I was still convinced that we would not be able to win the biggest games that way.

But, I watched Cavan put three goals past us in the first-half of the Division Two final. We won by scoring four goals in the second-half. It was not a game that anyone had a heart to analyse afterwards. It was too bizarre. Ridiculous in parts, too. We led 0-12 to 3-2 at half-time. Of their five scores in the half, one was from a free. So, they had four scores in total from play and we had blitzed them, and we still ended up virtually level pegging. They'd led 2-1 to 0-1 after eight minutes, and we needed eight unanswered points to get our noses back in front by the interval.

Niall Kilroy and David Murray scored two goals to put the scoreboard right. But there was still only one point in it with 18 minutes remaining. Cathal Cregg slid the ball under their goalkeeper, Raymond Galligan for our third goal, but we were still stuck in a game of cat and mouse. Seanie Johnston cut the gap to two. The nail in Cavan's coffin was our fourth goal from Conor Devaney.

REPEATEDLY, WE HAD given Cavan a lifeblood.

That was my reading of the game, and I did not need to pour over hours of analysis to know that that was the case.

One of their goals was one of our defenders falling off a tackle. 'Pawing' as I told our lads more than once. Pawing, and not stopping an opponent, and sending him in reverse with a proper hit.

'Pawing…

'Pawing!'

The best teams were seeing that, and they also viewed us being opened up in Croke Park like a tin of tomatoes just purchased off the shelf… and hey presto!

I tried not to think about this too much.

I knew, however, that other managers would look at the game before they were due to meet us and they would tell their players that there were goals, lots of goals available to them against Roscommon. All they had to do was run down the throat of our defence.

Promotion had taken huge pressure off me personally. I had spoken to the county board about developing our squad while we were down in Division Two. But they knew, as I did, that financially, and as a football brand, we needed to be back in Division One and there could be no excuse for not getting back there in double quick time.

We needed Division One.

For our sponsors. For the eyes of Roscommon people. For our self-esteem, and any future notion of our true self-worth. Everything had ridden on getting back up. I did not like what I had seen at any time in the whole league campaign, and I was shuddering at large doses of the Division Two final, but I was a happy man.

We had a seven weeks break before the start of the championship. I knew that we had played a risky strategy through the spring but, by early summer, we'd be a whole different team to the Roscommon team that had made Cavan look as slick and creative as a Kerry or a Dublin team at full speed.

All was as good as it possibly could have been, but the fact that we would be without Sean Mullooly, our best defender, pound for pound our best player, was only now fully revealing itself to me. Sean was one of our leaders. He led from the front, both in the privacy of the gym and out on the field. He told me midway through the league campaign that he was heading to the United States for the summer.

The story of Roscommon!

He called me to tell me. We didn't meet up. The call came out of the blue, and midway through I realised that Sean was not for turning.

He was more than one of our best men. He was a genuinely lovely lad whom everyone liked. He was great fun, and he was also a bull of a man on the ball. He was just a superb all round athlete, and a rarity in the county. He was such a beautiful hand-passer. His timing with those passes was always impeccable. He was able to take the ball on and get forward with serious intent. All of this, and I had to turn around and inform the rest of the lads in the room that a real opportunity had now opened up for… 'someone else in this room'.

Liam had built so much around Mullooly as he primed and coached the team. In the 2017 Connacht final it was Mullooly, when it truly mattered, who drove everyone else on, and who would always either win a loose ball or be next to the man in the primrose jersey who gobbled it up. He could cover ground, and Liam and I had spoken about him breaking off our midfielders in 2018, and going!

As I spoke in the dressing-room about life after Sean in 2018, I could almost see the stars from the blow to the chin I had taken when I answered Sean's phone call.

16

GALWAY 0-16 ROSCOMMON 2-6
CONNACHT SFC FINAL
ROSCOMMON
JUNE 17

AS WE DID a damned good job of making Cavan look fairly spectacular as an attacking threat, Galway were entertaining Dublin the same afternoon in Croke Park. And Galway made a statement.

They lost, but they had a big say in the Division One league final.

Kevin Walsh had certainly not shied away from emphasising to his players how vitally important it was to stay in Division One and, a bit like us in 2016, they made sure to be a step or two ahead of every single team they met. They were unbeaten in their seven divisional games. Two weeks before the Division One final they had hosted Dublin in Salthill and fought them to a draw.

Galway remained in fighting mood.

It was obvious to me that, in some respects, they were looking past us, and Mayo aswell. Galway clearly had designs on becoming a Croke Park team. Historically the county has always been quite at home in Croker. Walsh wanted to play to that legacy, and resurface Galway's standing as one of the game's superpowers.

Dublin would win their fifth league title in six seasons, winning by four points, 0-18 to 0-14, but they had to pay a price for it. James McCarthy limped out of the game in the first-half with a hamstring injury, and after the interval Paul Mannion and Michael Darragh Macauley had to leave the field after receiving hard knocks.

Damien Comer was the man who told Dublin they were in for a long afternoon. In the first 20 minutes of the game he stayed inside, on the edge of the square, in an orthodox full-forward role and he had scored one point, and had been fouled for three of Barry McHugh's free-kicks. He was marked by Philly McMahon who was also on a yellow card by the end of that 20 minutes.

Galway looked the real thing.

At 0-9 each at the change the final looked poised. Galway had stood up to Dublin physically. And tactically they had gone toe-to-toe with Jim Gavin and his brain trust.

But Dublin rattled off three points in two minutes when the two teams reappeared. Brian Howard and Brian Fenton asserted themselves in the middle third. Dublin had Niall Scully sent off after receiving a second yellow card. Galway did not appear in the second-half with the same fight or big desire.

Watching Galway take a step back helped me accept my entire day in Croke Park.

IN THE MIDDLE of February, we had beaten Galway in the FBD League final in the Hyde, and it was important that we did so. Even if we turned the screw from the 2017 Connacht final just that tiny amount.

Galway and ourselves in 2018, any time we met was going to be a game of inches. Kevin Walsh and myself both understood that. Galway know that Roscommon traditionally hold only the most basic amount of respect for those maroon jerseys. There is no fear or doubt, or second-guessing which is the case on too many occasions when Roscommon share a field with Mayo.

Both teams were understrength, but it did not matter. We won. We led early, building a 0-4 to 0-0 lead after 10 minutes. Enda Smith had won the throw-in and he fed his brother, Donie with a ball that bounced in front of him, and Donie swivelled onto his left for his score. Cathal Cregg got two points, one off either foot, and in between Ross Timothy raced forward from centre-back and took his own score.

They scored two goals against the run of play, and were one up at half-time. Moving Enda Smith to full-forward put us back in command. He scored a great individual goal, and although Galway kept plugging away we did enough with a point from Niall Daly and two more from Diarmuid Murtagh. I'd brought Diarmuid into the game near the end. I wanted us to have a right good cut at it, once the game was there to be won or lost near the finish.

2-16 to 3-12.

It was a scoreline, however, that warned us of the defensive inadequacies we would observe right through the league. But we'd beaten Galway. Again. And if we met again in the summer, that FBD final win would be twice as significant for us.

Maybe not for them.

But for us, it was just sweet enough.

Once the Connacht final came into view, I knew that there was more at stake for Kevin Walsh. Less for me in our personal duel. We'd won one final each, and Galway folk were not prepared to watch their team going down to us a second time. Defeat in a third final was going to leave Walsh wobbling. Or maybe gone before very long.

I had never imagined my time with Roscommon doubling as a personal duel between myself and Kevin Walsh. I like him, and respect him, and at the end of games he is as decent as they come in accepting any result.

But, I knew that Roscommon had been a lingering problem for him. When he was managing Sligo back in 2010 and they had brilliantly fought their way to the Connacht final by seeing off both Mayo and Galway, a dream provincial win was stopped in its tracks when Roscommon were one point a better team in the final.

If we followed up our 2017 win with a second Connacht title at Galway's expense, I don't believe people would have been prepared to listen to any explaining from their manager. I think the job of work that Kevin Walsh was attending to would have broken up. If Galway fell back from No.2 to No.3 in the west?

The two of us were back in the final, but we both understood that the prize on offer was No.2. Nobody doubted Mayo's right, whether they won the Connacht title or not, to be seen as No.1.

FIRST, WE HAD to beat Leitrim.

We would do so, 0-24 to 0-10, but Carrick-on-Shannon always holds some legitimate fears for Roscommon teams. We had to be exactly right. And stop them, which we did successfully for 39 minutes when they did not manage to score. It was 0-8 to 0-2 at the break. It was also an afternoon when we could stand back on the sideline and take some delight in being the bigger, more imposing team physically.

The loss of Sean Mullooly was calmed that little bit by having Cathal Compton back with us and fit. He was the most natural midfielder we had in the county, and partnering him with Tadhg O'Rourke gave us a powerful platform. Compton also allowed us to move Enda Smith to No.12, which is Enda's more natural position.

Compton is also a proper midfielder, who knows how to spoil the opposition. He understands the mechanics of the position, and he is blessed with two great feet. I knew he would be absolutely vital to us in the fight in the middle third against Galway, and perhaps gain a vital advantage when it mattered most.

GALWAY HAD A more stubborn look to them in 2018, and that was because they had Paddy Tally training them. Tally was not there for his flamboyancy.

But Tally was a proven operator, having done his part with Tyrone successfully in 2003 and also helping an average enough Down team to an All-Ireland final appearance in 2010. I knew Tally would have watched us as closely as anyone else. We'd been the league's top scorers, with an average of 19 points per game.

Himself and Walsh would also have gorged themselves on the opening to the 2017 Connacht final, when we pushed up on Ruairi Lavcelle's kick-outs, and left them sufficiently panicked. Those classy early points and Cian Connolly's goal had us 1-6 to 0-2 in front after 14 minutes.

Our strategy was perfectly conceived.

Its execution was also exact, and Tally and Walsh would also be telling themselves that we did the same to Mayo in the drawn game in the All-Ireland quarter-final when we hit the front after 10 minutes on a 2-2 to 0-01 scoreline.

They'd see us for what we were, and what we liked to do. The last thing they would want was to give us space in their half of the field. Tally and Walsh knew what our men could do in space. We were as good as anybody from inside or from distance. I knew Galway respected us. In fact, it would have been better if they respected us a little less.

Obviously, they were also looking back at their defeat to Dublin with some regret because they had failed to push on after that impressive opening 35 minutes. Against Mayo, in the Connacht quarter-final, they had shown that they had learned from that, and in their 21 point win over Sligo in the semi-final they finely tuned their intentions to balance a big defensive game with a furious counter-attacking game.

Tally's fingerprints were all over Galway's performance in that win over Mayo in MacHale Park. They remained rigid in their tactical formation, and were prepared to go point for point with Mayo for the full 70 minutes. If a team actually went out to play for a draw in a game of football, then Galway could stand accused of doing exactly that. Their winning goal from Johnny Heaney came in the fifth minute of injury time.

ONCE AGAIN, I had Niall McInerney match up on Comer.

I felt as good about that decision as I had 12 months before, and the only slight risk was our choice of Fintan Cregg at No.6. We wanted him filling the position like Sean Mullooly filled it. Fintan did not let us down either.

We had the game deconstructed to our advantage, I felt.

And by half-time I was doubly sure that I was making better choices than Kevin Walsh. We were a goal to the good, 1-5 to 0-5, and we had a strong breeze at our backs awaiting us in the second 35 minutes.

Media reports the next day were right in their criticism of our second-half performance. We lacked that touch of certainty, and there were three or four critical passes that we did not execute. We got points, but we could have got another goal if we had one more perfect pass. I wanted that extra pass.

I wanted goals.

Goals, and I was sure that we would beat Galway.

I watched *The Sunday Game* analysis of our shot choices the next day, and once, twice, three times, four times, I watched one of our men shooting for his point when, inside him, there was another pass on. And I struggled to understand how it had happened, and how it had repeated itself.

WATCHING, I ALSO could not help myself thinking of Sean Mullooly. He would have melted Shane Walsh's head. Walsh would have known that Mullooly was ready to bomb forward. He would have known Mullooly would have gone through him if necessary at the start of each of those runs.

Fintan Gregg is a classier footballer than Sean. But Fintan is not a big presence, like Sean. It's not that I wanted Fintan there for *presence*. I wanted him to be creative in the centre-back position and to work as a playmaker for us.

My firmest belief remained that if a lad is a great footballer then he should be able to fill most positions. Centre-back was a stretch for Fintan but we had played him there for a number of weeks to get him used to the role.

He did as well for us in the final as he possibly could have done. Shane Walsh ended the game with eight points. Five of them were from frees. I don't regret for one second choosing Fintan Cregg for No.6.

IN MY THREE years, the 2018 Connacht final is one match that I always look back on and never change my mind about it.

It was the one that *got away*.

A win would have made all the difference for us. And for me? A win would have meant that I carried on as manager, despite my personal issues. I'm sure my friends might have told me to take a rest for four or five months, but I would have been back for a fourth year, and maybe a year or two more after that.

Back-to-back victories over Galway in Connacht finals would have broken new ground for the county. Often enough during the year I had exchanged texts with Marty McDermott, who was the last man to do successive Connacht wins as Roscommon manager. Marty had stayed in the job for four years.

I always said to him... "We do the two in-a-row... I'll do four years minimum."

IF WE HAD beaten Galway, we would not have been in with Tyrone, Donegal and Dublin in our Super 8s grouping, either. We'd have been in the easier grouping. With Kildare who were flaky by the end of the summer. And Kerry who were also uncharacteristically flaky.

We would have performed better in the Super 8s.

Even if we didn't get through our grouping, I'd have received the benefit of the doubt from Roscommon supporters. I'd have figured a way to stay on, I'm sure. It might not have been good for me, but I would have looked to stay. And see what might happen next, in 2019?

The glory game of my three years was the 2017 Connacht final.

The defining game was 2018.

Losing to Kevin Walsh and Galway.

THE FIRST-HALF was close to perfection for us.

Galway had 13 men behind the ball. They were not bothered pressing high at our end. Even though they had Paddy Tally on board, I was surprised at their refusal to really work the wind that was at their backs.

They allowed us to press.

We forced turnovers, and they were rightly panicked by the time the 35 minutes ended and we led 1-5 to 0-5. I was never prouder of our lads in that half. I wish I could have said the same about the second 35 minutes when they failed to deliver those absolutely vital inside passes.

We were so calm, and so intelligent in the half. We waited, and we never lost patience. Diarmuid Murtagh was magnificent inside, deep in the Galway stranglehold. He was so decisive in his judgment, and he was also receiving perfect ball from Enda Smith. We were also making cutting runs that were timed to precision, and from one such bold surge Ciaráin Murtagh got inside Barry McHugh and raced across the end-line before hitting the back of the net.

DIARMUID MURTAGH KICKED the first point of the second-half to make it a four-point game. We had them beaten. However, they saved their own necks by coming out for the second-half with a determination to press high up the field.

They knew it was their only shot.

Walsh and Comer up front, and Ian Burke starting to buzz into space, gave them options when they won ball in the middle third.

They looked dangerous, but we had the ball and the chances to finish them off before they made one final mighty effort.

Donie Smith shot wide when the pass was on inside.

Diarmuid Murtagh did the same.

Then Niall Kilroy.

And Fintan Cregg.

Four chances to score points if the pass had gone inside. An inside pass and we would have had glorious chances of goals, too.

WE DID NOT manage one score from play in the final 35 minutes, and in the time added on. We scored one goal from a penalty, and a solitary free-kick.

Galway hit us for 11 points.

IN OUR HUDDLE out on the field, before going back to our dressing-room at half-time, Liam and Ger and I had not taken long to clarify exactly what we wanted to tell the lads inside.

They had played the perfect half of football.

They had played exactly the way we had asked them to play.

Change nothing.

Keep playing the ball wide and then, when you shift across the field, shift at speed. Fast, jabby hand-passing. Change nothing.

Keep that quick foot-passing.

Bring their defence over to one side, bring them back to the other side, keep bringing them over and back. Someone in their line in defence will lose it. Wait for them to make the mistake. Then cut inside.

Change absolutely nothing.

WE HAD BEEN playing like Dublin. Exactly like the greatest team in the modern game, because we had decided to model our search for scores on how Jim Gavin's team went about slowly, slowly and them quickly dismantling defences. Stretching and stretching those defences, until there is a tear, and then a hole in those defences.

NOTHING ON?

Skim it across to the far side of the field. Probe there. Still nothing on?

Bring it back. Quickly.

Can we get a central player coming through at speed?

Someone coming off the shoulder powerfully?

Galway had played right into our hands in the first-half. They had men in pockets in their defence marking space.

The only real way for those Galway players to stay in the game was to follow the ball, and following the ball is not a natural form of good defending.

The ball might be there.

But the man who is about to get onto the ball is more important. Galway were not following our men who were about to get onto the ball, and who were going to cause that tear in their defensive wall.

GALWAY, IN THAT first-half, were guilty of awful handling.

They were giving the ball away very easily to us, and their foot-passing was just as poor. They were unable to build any momentum throughout the field, and when they looked to get Comer on the ball deep in our defence they sent in long, skidding passes that were 20 yards to his left or to his right, that were zipping over the end-line.

THEY CHANGED ALMOST everything in the second-half. We went flat. But we had a chance to change it all back in the 67th minute when we were awarded a penalty. We were not playing well and, incredibly, we had a penalty that was going to put us ahead again.

On the sideline, however, we did not pay much attention to the penalty.

Liam and Ger and I were more worried about getting all our men back into the right positions for after the penalty. We wanted all of our lads not to be watching the penalty. We wanted them thinking about the kick-out.

Liam was on the field, roaring instructions.

I wasn't worried about the penalty. I knew that Conor Devaney would do what Conor does, and I had no doubt that he would execute it with total conviction. I did not expect him to hit it into the top left hand corner, with curl for some good measure.

It was a magnificent penalty.

It was the most critical kick in our three years together as a group of people, but the kick-out, we knew, would be even more important.

We knew we faced a kick-out that would be a thousand times more important than any other kick-out in the whole three years. It was a kick-out that I expected to win the Connacht title for us, again.

Get this, I told myself... *we'll get fouled, or we'll get a shot off.*

Get this... Galway are done!

THE KICK WAS taken and...

Two of our lads had lost concentration. They were not where they were supposed to be.

The ball was on the 20 metres line.

One of their defenders took off on a run right across the field, and Conor got lost in the moment. He had stopped. *He was taking the penalty. How could Conor have heard anything we were roaring?*

In the confusion after his kick, he lost his man.

Galway, like us, had a Connacht final depending entirely on one kick-out. All of their hard work in turning the game back in their favour in the second-half no longer mattered. All that mattered was that kick from their goalkeeper.

And they were smart.

They ran the right play, and they beat us because of a kick-out.

Kevin Walsh got me.

He got me with one kick from his own 20 metres line.

IT WAS CERTAINLY the game that got away.

My one massive regret.

At half-time, I told myself that we had it. We were a goal up, and in our dressing-room I could hear the roaring and shouting next door.

Actually, the wall dividing the two dressing-rooms in Hyde Park does not hit the ceiling flush and there is a four inch gap at the very top.

In our dressing-room we all knew about that gap. We could hear them shouting in the Galway dressing-room. If we all quietened, we could hear almost everything.

Though we never did quieten in the room. We had too much to do and say ourselves. We just lowered our own voices whenever we spelled out our most important orders and demands. At other times, we'd shout and roar as a group and make sure our opponents got to hear us revving things up.

I'd heard the Galway team coming in. I could hear voices getting louder and louder. I did not hear Kevin Walsh, but I heard enough to know that they were in a bad place.

We had them in trouble.

We had them.

And we let them go.

EPILOGUE

THERE WAS A two week wait, at the tail end of the summer of 2018, before we played Dublin in our final game in the Super 8s. The atmosphere in training was terrible.

Nothing sinister, just a deadbeat attitude.

We all suffered from it, players and management.

'It's Croke Park...

'It's Dublin...

'What a great place to finish our season!' I told everyone.

Except, our season was already over. We were eliminated from the Super 8s after losing to Donegal.

'Let's not let ourselves down, lads!' I implored.

Privately, I had agreed with Liam and Ger that we'd enjoy our final day out in 2018. We'd have a cut at it.

No defensive bolloxology. We'd play our game, we'd play ball.

EXCEPT, OF COURSE, I was not going to be part of it all.

My performance in the first-half of the Donegal game in the Super 8s with the linesman, and my ball throwing expertise at half-time, resulted in a charge of 'minor physical interference' with a match official.

The Central Controls Competition Committee banned me for 12 weeks. I thought the three months excessive. We've all seen men on the sideline lamp someone on the opposite team and get less than three months.

I heard about the suspension on the Wednesday morning after we'd lost to Donegal. I told Brian Carroll, our county secretary, that I would not be appealing.

I even made it known that I would drive up to Dublin, for our final round game against Dublin in the Super 8s, in my own car. I had talked Verona and my daughters out of coming to the game. It had been a long enough season for them.

I'd drive up to Dublin alone.

I wasn't allowed to be anywhere near the team, and I was willing to go by the letter of GAA law. Everyone else said I was mad.

I arrived at Hyde Park on the Sunday in my car, but didn't park it alongside all of the other cars. 'I'm driving!' I reminded Liam and Ger, and the county board officials. I was determined to drive, and meet up with the team in the Crowne Plaza Hotel in Santry.

I didn't want any more controversy.

A circus, with me in the centre of the ring, getting more attention than the match about to be played was the last thing required, I felt.

'I'm driving!'

'You're not!'

They wouldn't hear of it.

I was bundled onto the team bus in the end. But I still could not be seen anywhere near the team once we got up close to Croke Park. I'd chatted with Sean Mulryan, one of our great sponsors, in the middle of the week.

Sean told me I could make myself at home in the Ballymore box in the ground.

ONE OF THE many great men who pours himself into a supportive role with the Roscommon football team is Shay Wade. He's a taxi man in the city, and a true blue Dub. And he looks after all our Dublin-based players.

Shay is an amazing individual. A lovable man. I had phoned him earlier in the week and he agreed that he would meet me at the hotel. We'd venture in the direction of Croke Park together, a suitable distance behind the team bus.

◊ ◊ ◊ ◊ ◊

BY THE CLOSE of 2018, I was simply exhausted.

After we lost to Dublin, 4-24 to 2-16, and the whole season finally wrapped itself up, I was ready to lie down for several days. But there were things to do.

Fairly instantly, we had to begin the process of preparing for the 2019 season and, although short of energy, I was ready to go on, and take on whatever had to be done to make Roscommon feel comfortable in the role of one of the country's top eight football teams.

If we headed back into the Super 8s, I wanted us not to feel like an outsider, like we had felt in 2018.

IN EARLY SUMMER of 2018, in late May, my doctor John Keenan had told me that my PSA levels were a little too high for his liking.

Because I am over 50, I get my bloods checked every year. I'm not a great eater, and working as a football manager, and also working around the clock with RTE at weekends, it was the easiest thing to load absolute rubbish into my diet. Verona knew my cholesterol was higher than it should have been. Texaco stations and the canteen in RTE were not servicing me properly, my wife advised me more than once.

I knew that myself. When you are a manager of a football team invariably you believe that everyone else's health and welfare in the dressing-room is more important than your own.

Too many biscuits, too many dodgy sandwiches, far too much coffee. At the start of 2018, Doctor Keenan told me that if I did not 'tidy myself up' that he'd have to put me on statins for my cholesterol. He gave me three months.

He told me to go out walking.

He told me to lose some weight.

And I felt good when I reported back to the doctor's surgery. John Keenan wasn't alarmed by the PSA levels. Neither was I. He said it was highly unlikely to be anything but, at the same time, he said he could not rule out something.

An appointment was made with a specialist in the Bon Secours in Galway, who told me we could live with the levels, but suggested an MRI. Three days later, on a dirty, filthy Saturday afternoon in Roscommon town, as a result of a late cancellation I got a call to say they could take me in for the scan.

I was there by 7.0 pm.

The MRI was showing shadows.

Nothing conclusive, I was assured. But the specialist wanted a biopsy. He knew by the look on my face that I was pretty certain that the biopsy was not on page one of my list of priorities. The championship was about to commence.

We agreed on August, when the football season was about over for Roscommon. I left it at that. Though I was slightly concerned. Everybody had said that I was probably fine, but nobody had said that I was absolutely fine.

◊ ◊ ◊ ◊ ◊

SHAY AND I drove down Clonliffe Road, and turned to approach the back of the Hogan Stand. We were stopped by the big, raised arm of the law.

'Where the hell do ye think ye'r going!'

Shay had a residents pass on him. But Shay is one of those men who does not like to reach for his very last resort. 'I'm just dropping off the Roscommon team manager... at the back of the stand over there,' he told the garda.

I also strained my head across, and said a polite 'hello'.

'Who?'

The garda was not in the mood for someone trying to get one over him. 'Have ye ID?' he asked. 'Have ye a pass or anything?'

Shay said he did not.

'But I do have the Roscommon team manager here, right next to me,' Shay continued. '... Kevin McStay!'

The garda stooped lower to have a good look at me.

I smiled back at him.

'I don't care who you have with you!' he announced.

Shay produced his resident's pass.

The garda remained doubtful, and got on his radio and had a quick chat with the invisible and great garda in the sky.

'He says... he's the Roscommon team manager!'

I GOT TO the Ballymore box two hours before the start of the match. There was a lovely mix of people there, made up of sound Roscommon folk. One of my best friends and the team logistics man, Sean Finnegan was there, and Sean saw to it that after a beautiful bite to eat, and possibly the best food I'd had on the road in several years, that I was wired up to Liam and Ger down on the sideline.

It was a strange and weird experience. I was surrounded by friends. Sean Mulryan, of course. Seamus Hayden and Tony McManus were there, two fantastic Roscommon men and two men who were one hundred per cent supportive of me, and brilliantly loyal. Seamus was always a calm advisor, astute across so many of the relevant topics – the football, and the politics of football. He was just rock solid.

We watched as the team put up its biggest score of the whole season against the three-times and about to be four-times All-Ireland champions. Two goals. And 16 points. Even if Dublin were moving down the gears through the afternoon, it was a decent performance, and we also got to give two of our team's greatest servants, Sean McDermott and Ian Kilbride a proper farewell by getting them onto the field by the end. They were both retiring. They deserved one last bow in front of the Roscommon supporters, and there was no better stage than Croke Park.

I, however, did not get to go into the team dressing-room after the match. I had no idea that I had watched Roscommon for the last time as the county manager.

IT WAS ALL about to end, and faster than I had ever imagined.

It was my own fault that I was not in the dressing-room.

A moment with the players would have been nice in that room. I felt bad about it afterwards, when I thought about it. On the team bus, I caught up with a few of the lads, but others were spending the night in the city and deservedly pulling closed the curtains on a long season.

I felt I had let them down.

I had let myself down.

Slobbering on the sideline against Donegal, as my late father would definitely have viewed it.

◊ ◊ ◊ ◊ ◊

IN THE DAYS that followed, back home in Roscommon, it was time for talking about the future. I would talk with the players representing the whole squad. I would talk with the county board. I was also talking with other people. I had met with Donie Buckley, the specialist defensive coach who had left the Mayo set-up. I wanted us to become a stronger unit.

First of all, I sat down with Ger Dowd.

We met in the Comfy Cafe on the main street in Roscommon, not our usual meeting spot. Rogue and Co was too busy, and Ger and I wanted a quieter conversation. We had a long chat over several coffees.

A few hours later, Verona and I were due down in Sean Mulryan's beautiful home, in Ballymore Eustace in Kildare, where there was a dinner party, more of a banquet really, that Sean was holding as usual, on the Friday before the All-Ireland final. It was always a magnificent event.

Sean Mulryan is a great, generous man, and thankfully he is a Roscommon man as well. Tom Hunt and Sean, anything we ever wanted during our three years with the team was simply never a problem to them. As sponsors they were aware, and quietly at hand. Verona and I were going to spend the weekend in Dublin. We had tickets for the game on the Sunday. A long, enjoyable two days lay in front of us.

I had barely shut the door of the Comfy Cafe behind me, when I tumbled.

The heel of my shoe had got caught in a hole in the footpath, and I hit the ground in an instant. My right ankle went up like a balloon. Serious ligament damage. As I fell forward, I had also landed on my head and shoulder.

Ger had turned to see me go down.

Ollie McGuinness, the pharmacist on the street whom I had also trained when he played with Roscommon Gaels, came running out of his shop.

He took over operations.

And, amazingly, I looked up to see a woman in her 30s take out her mobile phone and point it in my direction as I lay there, crumpled up on the footpath awaiting the ambulance.

'You're not going to do, what I think you're going to do?' I asked her.

'Are you?'

She put the phone away and scooted off.

Verona was quickly on the scene too. She saw me lying there. Ollie had placed some jacket under my head. Verona knew I was pretty okay, but everyone else around the town was quickly being told that Kevin McStay had a heart attack… a stroke… a brain haemorrhage.

I was on my way to Tullamore hospital before I knew it, in the company of two ambulance men who were also great Rossie football supporters. The consultant on duty in the hospital, Sean O'Rourke, was an Offaly GAA man and he got me turned around with crutches. By 5.0 o'clock I was home.

I watched Dublin defeat Tyrone in the All-Ireland final from the near perfect seat in my own sitting room on the Sunday afternoon.

◊ ◊ ◊ ◊ ◊

ON THE TUESDAY evening before my fall on the street, I had sat down with our captain, Conor Devaney and Diarmuid Murtagh. The two of them, and David Murray who could not attend on the night, represented the players as a group. The three of them especially were made of the right stuff. They were massively ambitious and were not prepared to allow anything to stand in the way of Roscommon becoming the No.1 team in Connacht.

The management team met in the Abbey Hotel earlier that evening, about 5.0 pm. But I also needed an assessment of the season from our players, who joined us three hours later. I wanted to know what they were thinking about everything that had happened, and I wanted their thoughts on 2019.

I wanted warts and all.

It was what was needed. We all needed to be big boys in the room.

We had a good chat. We got bare and honest thoughts, and some feedback that was fairly raw, some of it unforgiving. Over an hour and a half had passed quickly enough. A recognised defensive coach was at the top of the list we got from Conor and Diarmuid. Players' expenses were on the list. It was a proper list. Getting their team kit early was mentioned. A warm weather training week early in 2019 was requested. There were no real surprises, and I was impressed at how Conor had his report detailed on his laptop. Then, Conor said something else.

About a few lads retiring. About a few lads going away.

He said it casually enough.

'Ahhhh... Jesus!

'Who's going away?'

I was stunned. Conor had just told us that some of the lads were going to take time out from the squad. He named a few names. They needed to do other things in their lives.

But he wasn't sure how many were going to take off.

Or who was going, for certain.

'Conor... you're codding me!

You have to get back... to... EVERYONE.

'We need to know... we need to know straight away. How can we plan for next season when we don't know for sure who we have?'

I left the meeting in a ball of uncertainty. There had been six or seven issues that I was unhappy with to begin with, that I needed to try to get straightened out with the county board. And now, on top of that, I had players who wanted a long break.

Jaysus lads.

Do none of ye get it?

I had to keep my thoughts to myself, but they were thoughts that were drilling around in my head constantly.

We're going back into Division one.

We need everyone... and we need... EVERYTHING RIGHT THIS TIME.

We know we're not good enough... right now!

And we know what we need to do... to change!

CAN WE CHANGE?

AS A MANAGEMENT team, we had already begun a root and branch check through the whole squad. It was decision time.

We knew we were at a crossroads as a group.

It was time to identify the serious movers and shakers on the team. Circle the names of the strongest characters. We also had to draw lines through the names of players who simply did not have it in them, for different reasons, to step up to the highest level of the game.

Some of the players Conor Devaney had suggested were ready to take off for 12 months were these players. Lads we were going to have to let go.

And that was okay.

But, Conor had also named two or three players, who were amongst the clutch of players we had identified as absolutely essential to Roscommon reaching the higher level, and gaining a proper foothold there.

They were some of our best lads... our best trainers. Lads who never landed a single issue or doubt on us.

I had asked Conor to get back to everyone in the next 24 hours and find out everything I needed to know. We were at a place and time, after our three years, where there was nowhere to hide for anybody, players or team management. Total honesty. And after that, complete dedication. If there was not total commitment to gym work and aerobic improvement, for starters, then there was nothing more that we could accomplish with the group.

The moment had arrived.

For us all. I knew who had not done the work asked of them. So also did our best and most ambitious players. The numbers were always there. David Joyce, and every good strength and conditioning expert, can provide any number of metrics. Those numbers do not lie.

Liam and I agreed that we had to start becoming ruthless. That was one missing ingredient amongst us as a management team.

We'd given everyone a fair crack at it for three years. There was no point in sustaining the myth that some of the lads could become high quality county footballers, or that some others would change their spots and work their arses off far away from the field.

Liam and Ger and I had built a group of footballers who were happy in each other's company, and enjoyed being part of the Roscommon dressing-room, and we had seen that as something very important. Friendships were so important.

But, in the future, Liam and Ger and I could no longer be everyone's friends.

I RECEIVED THE names, and I spoke to all of the players who were of a mind to take time out. Both the players I was not too concerned about, and critically the ones we could not do without.

I respected everything they told me.

Some of the conversations were brilliant, even if they were disappointing. There was real warmth and honesty there. The reasons presented to me were legitimate, even if it was a player wanting to take a year out for himself in America.

It wasn't just an itch to travel.

They had exams to concentrate on, degrees to be nailed down, new jobs and new directions in their lives.

◇ ◇ ◇ ◇ ◇

LEAVING IS NEVER all that easy.

Seldom do all the planets align, and allow you to smoothly walk away, with no doubts or distractions, no regrets.

When the time came for me to resign as Roscommon manager after serving for three seasons I did so with the heaviest heart. I had weighed it up for several days, and slept on it one more night before making the phone calls I needed to make the following morning.

Leaving the army after almost 32 years was not easy. As I have already stated, joining the army and leaving the army were two of the best decisions I made in my life but, still, it was not easy to turn my back on my military life.

AFTER MY CADETSHIP my life in the army began firstly and briefly in McKee Barracks and then Collins Barracks in Dublin. I was an officer. I was a Second Lieutenant which, in effect, meant that like all of the other Cadets who were commissioned, I had jumped five ranks.

All of us still young pups, with everything to learn, but pups who had jumped all the non-commissioned ranks, Private, Corporal, Sergeant, Company Sergeant and Sergeant Major. The day a Cadet gets those pips he or she gets saluted by a Sergeant Major, a real soldier, who might be 30 years older.

The Sergeant Major knows everything.

The brand new Second Lieutenant knows nothing much.

The trick is to know that you know nothing much, and to watch and listen, and learn and never stop learning from those who have served practically their entire lives.

MOST OF My friends were commissioned into the Infantry Corps. I went into the Signal Corps and spent my whole army career there.

In the next 30 years I was a full Lieutenant, a Captain, a Commandant and, finally, a Lieutenant Colonel. I rose through the ranks. I believe I could have gone further. People, I know, imagine that I have 20 things listed down every day on a 'To Do' list, but that was never me. Lots of things in my life I stumbled upon. I became Roscommon manager because an opening appeared. I had never targetted that role, and neither did I join the army in order to strive to be Chief of Staff.

Things have happened for me in my football life and in my army life because, I guess, I am reasonably talented.

I DID NOT wish to leave the army when I did.

I felt my retirement was close enough at hand, and the time I had done was going to allow me to make that decision at the right time for me and my family.

And then, in the summer of 2013, I had to hurriedly decide. I wanted to complete another full 12 months in the army to maximise my pension entitlements and full gratuity, and that meant staying until July 2014.

But I did not stay.

In my time, I had completed three tours overseas. I went to Lebanon near the end of 1992 and again in 2001, and I did another six months tour in Kosovo through the winter of 2007 and spring of 2008 when the wet and the coldness presented itself every single day and my job as Camp Commandant was to oversee all of the logistics, all of the everyday needs, the equipment and communications, bedding, food, and warmth, for 260 people in Camp Clarke.

I had signed up for one last overseas trip before my planned retirement in July of 2014, and had applied to do so in the autumn of 2013. That was agreed, but in April of 2013, out of nowhere, I received official word that I was being dispatched to Lebanon. I got four weeks' notice.

Two of our girls were starting their Leaving Certificates, and I was totally committed to helping them prepare for their examinations. I was also contracted to RTE in my role on *The Sunday Game* and other things for the full summer. That's why the autumn 2013 trip was agreed by all in advance.

I was living in the barracks in The Curragh at that time. Five days and nights every week separated from my family, which is always tough on any family man. The barracks in Athlone had been down-sized, and I had been redeployed to The Curragh.

Barracks life was something I got used to, but never loved

But it was my choice to work for RTE for the last half of my adult life also, so I can not genuinely complain about having my family life swallowed up by my commitments.

My work with RTE regularly means staying overnight in Dublin on a Saturday and Sunday. My life in the army regularly meant living in barracks from Sunday night until Thursday night. Evenings in the barracks are not easy on anyone. You are with your work colleagues, but you are also alone. You go for runs, or walks, and you go to the cinema or whatever, just to pass the evenings. Barracks life has left more than one good man broken up by loneliness and alcohol.

HALF OF MY head was taken up with thoughts at different stages of making another rank, and hitting Colonel before my retirement. The other half was settling on retirement from the army sooner rather than later.

It felt right to do one last tour overseas, from October, 2013 to May, 2014, then take a month's holidays, and then tidy up my affairs and retire. To do something else with my life.

The order to go to the Lebanon, when it came, knocked those plans for six. My plans were wiped out. In the army there is a publication called the *Gazette*, which, when it is published, represents the army Bible. Whatever is published in the *Gazette*, happens.

It was published that I was going to be in the Lebanon within a month.

The dye was cast.

I was forced to act in my own interests and in the best interests of my wife and daughters, and I resigned. A year's salary gone. I also lost half of my gratuity. And there was no final overseas trip to finish off my army career.

Thirty-two years, almost. I felt I had been let down badly by my superiors and others.

I was out.

THE TRADITION IN the army is that you get a phone call from a member of the general staff the day before or the day you resign.

Nobody phoned me.

The day I retired was harder than I had imagined. I found it very emotional. I'd been up since six in the morning because I had to do the *Morning Ireland* sports chat with Des Cahill at 7.30 am, and again at 8.30 am.

My last day in The Curragh I had waited for nearly everyone to go home before getting into my Jeep. It was a Friday evening. I had let down the back seats, and had packed everything from my room and my office into the car. I began to drive away, but then I thought of the Cadet School, where it had all started for me, where 18 months of suffering and learning, and beating six inches of shoe leather into the tarmac, suddenly did not seem like a whole lifetime ago. I drove up to it one last time.

It was perfectly quiet.

Nobody shouting out orders. Mostly everyone had left three hours earlier, by 4.0 pm. I was sitting in my car, in my civilian clothing.

The army uniforms and clothing were in one of the larger boxes in the seat behind me. I took several deep breaths. I silenced the car, and sat there. And my head was flooded with so many competing thoughts, beginning and ending with my mother telling me to think of the army as a possible career.

Suggesting with a heavier tone than normal that I had to make something of my life outside of Ballina.

THE OVERSEAS TRIPS were events in my life that are treasures. They are the testing ground for everything an army man or woman learns. We largely live garrisoned, regimented lives for large portions of our careers. We're the insurance policy for the country, always preparing for whatever might need to be done.

Overseas is real army life.

My first time in Lebanon, I have to admit I found it scary in the beginning. There was shelling and shooting for two months. At critical times I had to make my way to the command bunker. The operational centre for the Battalion. There we had to ensure that everything was working. That everyone could talk, and that everyone had what they needed in order to do their job for the day.

It was a great first trip. For the first time I had my full platoon working with me, and everyone in the platoon had all of the qualifications necessary. The radio operators, riggers, the satellite man, every last person in the platoon was an expert in what they had to do. And everyone was there.

There were no late replacements, like back home. Nobody filling in for someone else at the last minute in a practice routine. No sickies. I had everything I needed to effectively do the job I was trained to do to my fullest potential.

It's not like being a football manager who looks through his dressing-room and realises he is short in so many important positions.

I had all the right men under my command. No excuses. Every day, it was a question of getting the job done, and getting the job done right.

Seeking perfection, almost every single day, with 22 men in my platoon, doing our jobs in a buffer zone, a parcel of land about five miles wide and separating two warring armies, Hezbollah and Israel, the latter on the high ground always looking down upon us. Irish, Norwegians, Swedes, Fijians, Nepalese... all of us in there effectively keeping them apart.

My second tour in Lebanon was to decommission the camp. At that time in 2001 the Irish were getting out of there, the Irish 89th Battalion was leaving the zone and it was a huge logistical operation, as right down to the final weeks and days of the six months tour we had to see to it that the Irish Battalion was doing what was required, but was also ready to up sticks on an appointed date.

Everything had to be brought home. Radios, phones, computers... hundreds of them. Equipment in forward areas had to be taken in hand. Aerials had to be stripped down. It was a wonderful, and more relaxed trip than the first, however, as both warring parties had agreed on a peaceful interlude.

Kosovo was different in every way to Lebanon.

Not just because of the coldness, but the dampness never let up and in horrendous temperatures of minus 14 and lower, I always had to worry about generators. I had to get my hands on a new one from Italy in the middle of the tour. And get it fast!

But, like Lebanon, it was fulfilling at the same time to be acting out in real life the job I was trained to do. All of us. Nobody can go absent on tour. Nobody can decide to go on the beer. Everyone does the job. If there are 10 people rostered for kitchen duty, then there are 10 people in the kitchen, and not three or four people trying to do the jobs of 10.

At the same time, you can not help wondering before and after each tour, what exactly is it all about?

A question of legacy strikes you repeatedly?

I left Ireland for that tour before Christmas in 2007.

The twins were young.

The car came to collect me at our home. My eldest girl, Emma crying with her Mum, waving goodbye from the front door.

I didn't really want to go.

WHEN MY PHONE rang after finishing up with Des Cahill, I was surprised. I did not recognise the number. I don't usually answer unknown numbers. For some reason, I did this time.

'Hello?'

'Hello there, Lieutenant Colonel McStay... how are you today?'

For a couple of seconds, I did not recognise the voice, and I had to confess... 'You have me now... don't know who this is!'

'Well... I hope you are standing to attention,' the voice instructed, '... this is your Taoiseach here!'

I spoke with Enda Kenny for several minutes. About my army life, and some football inevitably. I grew emotional once I realised who I was chatting with.

We ended the call, and I sat there. Crying. But happy, too. On my last day of service the Taoiseach wanted me to know I could change my mind. He would ensure I could end my military career in the manner I had planned. I declined his offer, and thanked him. My decision was made.

I was happier. Far happier.

Someone had called me to say thank you.

◊ ◊ ◊ ◊ ◊

I WORE A massive orthopaedic boot for a while, as I waited for my ankle to make its recovery. A couple of weeks passed. I was under the expert care of the Roscommon team physiotherapist, Aisling Creighton who is based in Carrick-on-Shannon.

I resigned as team manager on September 5.

I had been conscious for several days that I needed to arrive at a crystal clear decision. I was also conscious that the Roscommon county board would need adequate time to get a new manager.

The decision had been mine

There was no pressure from the Board. Equally, the players as a body were ready to knuckle down and look at trying to become a better football team in 2019. There were a handful of players who were unhappy with me. There are always a handful who would like to see the back of every manager in every county.

Normally, the majority of that small bunch are not getting the game time they feel entitled to getting. Though the whole squad had made it known that they wanted a dedicated defensive coach. They wanted to change, dramatically, the philosophy about the game Roscommon had played in 2018.

I knew that, and had that to consider.

There were other things on my mind. The resources available to the team, and the finances. There were still creditors around the senior team. People who were owed money in 2018. This was not any one person's fault, or the fault of the Board. The county was in dire financial straits. But there were people whom I had asked to come in and work with us who were owed money, and they had been waiting three and four months, and they were ringing me.

And I had no answers for them.

We had no centre of excellence in the county... we had no county training ground even, and would have to continue begging and borrowing from clubs. The intentions of everyone involved, from the county board down were so strong, but in reality Roscommon remained weak. The infrastructure remained completely inadequate for a team even thinking of living amongst the game's Super 8 teams.

I was so frustrated. The gym that we had used in 2018, for instance, was no longer available to us for some reason I barely grasped. We had decided that the squad should get back to work at the start of October. But, the one place that we needed more than anything was not available to us at the precise time when we would need to get cracking for 2019. We had eight or nine of the finest conditioned footballers in the country. We had another eight or nine who were well off that mark, and we had another group further back in the same queue.

We had identified all of these players.

We had decided how to go about changing it all. I was going to take the lads in mid-Roscommon. Liam was going to come from Ballina and take the lads in the north of the county. Twice and three times a week. We had it all down on paper, and ready to start into it.

I spoke to our chairman two or three times during the period in which I counted down to my resignation. His loyalty had been unreal to me. On the team bus, coming home after being trounced by Dublin in the final game in the Super 8s he had told me that he and the executive wanted me to take things forward for another two years.

He reminded me that we had hit our targets for the year.

We were back in Division One.

We reached the Connacht final, and the Super 8s.

He also kindly reminded me that the season had not ended as everyone would have wished, but that there was more work now to be done.

I told him how decent he was being.

'But, I'm not going to say yes,' I also informed him. 'We've got to go home, and think about an awful lot of things.'

◊ ◊ ◊ ◊ ◊

VERONA AND I decided we would take a week in the sun, in Spain, in early October. Four days before flying out I was driving to Carrick for another good session on my ankle with Aisling when, on possibly the straightest stretch of road in the whole of Roscommon, I was rear-ended.

I was driving from Tulsk to Elphin. I was driving in my prized, heavy BMW that I had rewarded myself with when I retired from the army. The jeep that hit me had a rally car attached to the back of it that the young man was delivering to Donegal.

It was an awful wallop.

I got out and looked at my beautiful car, now fairly ruined.

But I was okay. My neck and back would become painful within 24 hours, however, and I found myself back in the A and E department in Tullamore once again. But between my visits to hospitals for the checks on my prostate, and also my ankle, the staff on duty declined to x-ray me to see if there was any damage done. I had already taken on board more than sufficient amounts of radiation, it seemed.

'Can I go on holiday?' I asked the doctor.

I needed a holiday.

I got the nod from him.

◇ ◇ ◇ ◇ ◇

IT WAS HARDER for me than it was for Liam. Ger Dowd, also living locally, he felt what I was feeling, but Ger was not the manager.

I was the man who had to wear the bainisteoir bib.

It was me people looked to for the big answers, and it was me who was going to get his backside kicked, publicly and privately, if Roscommon took a step back from the achievements of 2018.

After assessing everything for days, and after talking to some of my best players who were leaving the squad, I understood that I could not promise the people of Roscommon, and I could not assure myself, that 2019 would not be a painful retreat.

That is why I resigned.

I didn't want to. I wished to achieve more but, in my heart, I knew it was not possible.

LIAM WENT HOME to Ballina every evening.

He had no real sense of the politics circling the county football team. But Ger and I were tuned into what people were thinking, and what they were demanding.

In a county like Roscommon there are lots of opinions, big and small, not just amongst the hardened and more casual supporters, but through all the clubs. I have to say that the clubs never dictated to me in the three years.

But, I had to do right by the clubs, and I had to have an understanding of public opinion. That is just life.

THE DECISION, WHEN it was made, was one that simply made sense. As a county Roscommon did not have the structures in place to fight it out with the biggest football teams in the country.

And, in taking that fight to those same teams over three years, my health had suffered. As I debated my future as a manager, I was still awaiting the results of my biopsy. I kept telling myself that I would be fine.

I would not be told that I had prostate cancer.

I had been of that same belief before receiving the results of my MRI, which had been inconclusive. I was remaining positive, but I could not hide from the fact that I was suffering from a form of exhaustion that I had never experienced before.

I could not hide that from Verona and my daughters.

Neither could I pretend that I was fit and able to throw myself into another year with the team. I understood better than most that Roscommon people want to do more than survive as a football team.

They want to thrive.

They want Division One football

They want the Super 8s, again and again. And the good people of Roscommon have had a habit of chopping the heads off football managers who do not deliver what the county desires.

I finally admitted to Verona one evening in our home that it was not possible. I could not meet the wishes of the county.

Too many things needed to be done.

Too many things were still out of line.

I could do no more. I told Verona that I was too tired. She told me to have one more good night's sleep, and then make a final decision. And that is what I did, and when I got up the next morning I made my coffee and soon got into the phone calls that had to be made.

I called as many people as I could, but I also needed to send a long message on our WhatsApp group to the players and backroom team.

My statement announcing my resignation to the people of Roscommon was a lengthy one. Others, and especially some journalists housed in Dublin, ridiculed me for the length of it, suggesting it was self-serving. I had written it the night before.

When I got up the next morning I saw no reason to edit it back.

I did not wish to leave any loose ends.

I wanted to explain myself to the people of Roscommon who had given me the precious opportunity of a lifetime.

Also, I wanted to explain myself to every single person who had contributed to our three years together. I especially wanted to thank them for the good days, days which had left us happier than we thought possible when we had started out on the three years journey.

I wanted to thank them for their dedication and commitment. I had a lot of big thanking to do.

I did not care if it took a little bit longer to read my statement. More than anything, I wanted everybody who read my statement to understand that Roscommon now needed to take its football team to the highest level, and gain a foothold there. Remain amongst the best. Be the best in Connacht. And enjoy life as a Super 8 football team.

I wanted to explain to people why I could not help further in that aim.

SHORTY AFTER STEPPING down, I received the biopsy results which were negative. I still believed that I had made the correct decision.

AND I STILL do.

Verona and I decided that we would give one another more time.

Quality time, it's formally called.

I would not work with RTE anymore, and not find myself running out of our home at the beginning of each weekend in the summer months, and not getting home for 24, maybe 36 hours later.

Neither would I manage any more football teams.

I would busy myself in other ways. I would write a newspaper column perhaps, if asked, and *The Irish Times* came around the corner in the early part of 2019 and I agreed to work with them.

I'd continue teaching maths, which is something I love doing, working with Higher Level Junior and Higher Level Leaving Certificate students and helping them through one of the most stressful periods of their lives for some. These classes give me such satisfaction and joy.

But no more football teams.

No more RTE.

Then the newly appointed Head of Sport in RTE, Declan McBennett called me and asked me to consider returning to *The Sunday Game*. My gut instinct was to stick to my guns, and say no thank you.

But I listened. I agreed, and for the summer of 2019 I found myself back in the RTE campus in Montrose in Dublin, and also back in football grounds all over the country at weekends. I found myself back, high up, in Croke Park. Looking down on football managers and their selectors and all of their helpers, and judging them.

Once upon a time, I thought I knew everything I needed to know about them and what they were attempting to do. But I didn't.

I did not know enough. But after three years on the Roscommon sideline I think I now know so much more. About them, and the game they are involved in.

A game unlike any other. A game of football which is different to the game their players are involved in, and a game quite alien to the game that is being watched and commented upon by supporters. And very often pundits!

There is one man down on the sideline who is in the middle of something quite unique. A game of football that never ends, a game that bounces from one weekend to the next. A game of football that he always wants to win.

But, also a game which he realises, will ultimately leave almost every single manager, every season without fail, a loser in the estimation of a vast number of people.

It's a great game, and a fun game. It's also a torturous game.

But one thing it always remains... and always has been...

The pressure game.